ARTISAN SOURDOUGH

Made Simple

A Beginner's Guide to Delicious
Handcrafted Bread with Minimal Kneading

Recipes and Photography by

Emilie Raffa

Author of *The Clever Cookbook* and
Creator of The Clever Carrot

PAGE STREET
PUBLISHING CO.

PAGE STREET
PUBLISHING CO.

This book is dedicated
to those who will continue to
share the powerful journey
of sourdough.

Contents

INTRODUCTION

Ever wonder how to bake sourdough, but don't know where to begin? I'm going to tell you a secret: You don't have to be a professional baker or have a concrete knowledge base to get started. Sourdough can be accessible to anyone. All you need are a few basic ingredients and tools, and I'll guide you the rest of the way.

So what is sourdough anyway? In a nutshell, sourdough is slow-fermented bread. What's unique is that it does not require commercial yeast in order to rise. It's made with a live fermented culture, a sourdough starter, which acts as a natural leavening agent. Now, if this concept sounds absolutely bizarre, don't worry, you're not crazy. I used to think it was some kind of mad science project myself. But in actuality, it's a technique that can be traced back thousands of years, before commercial yeast was available to bakers.

Sourdough is known for its delicious, complex flavor. It is not necessarily "sour" dough. The flavor can be either mild or tangy, depending on how the starter is cared for and how the dough is made. You won't find any hydrogenated oils, corn syrup, or preservatives lurking in homemade sourdough—it's 100% natural. As an added health benefit, the slow fermentation process breaks down the hard-to-digest proteins and enzymes found in wheat, which is why some people who are gluten-sensitive have reported being able to digest sourdough without any issues.

Interestingly enough, that's not what lured me into sourdough at all. I had been admiring the popular Australian blog Fig Jam and Lime Cordial, where Celia documented her experience with sourdough baking at home. Her style was so approachable that any time I read one of her posts, I thought to myself, "I want *that*. I want what she's having." And it wasn't about the bread, necessarily (although it looked incredible and I wanted to rip off a chunk right though the computer screen!). It was her enthusiasm, both sincere and infectious, that lured me in from the opposite side of the globe. Eventually, I built up enough courage to reach out and connect with her, which marked the beginning of an unexpected friendship.

As you can imagine, I nearly fell over when Celia asked, "Hey hon, do you want me to send you some of my sourdough starter?" Two weeks later, a small envelope dotted with Australian postage arrived at my doorstep. Inside was a plastic bag filled with tiny white flakes. How this peculiar-looking thing made it through customs was beyond me. But it didn't matter. This was Priscilla, Celia's sourdough starter.

One of the first things I learned is that sourdough is meant to be shared. Priscilla, almost 10 years old at the time of writing this book, has been shared all over the world. Her offspring can be found in the tiny kitchens of New York and the tallest buildings of Dubai. This spawned a family tree of bakers and new close friendships. What's fascinating is that each of us has welcomed Priscilla into our homes, making her unique to our own sourdough journey. We are living proof that anyone can adapt this ancient technique into modern-day life.

With my new sourdough starter in tow, I was ready to bake bread. Admittedly, the first few loaves that emerged from my tiny oven looked more like hockey pucks than anything edible. But eventually, my luck changed. Every now and then, I'd post a few pictures online or to my blog, The Clever Carrot, and inquiring minds wanted to know my formula. Formula? To my knowledge, sourdough was simple: Throw everything into a bowl, let it rise overnight, and walk away. No kneading. Basic shaping. It was just bread after all, right?

Naturally, curiosity kicked in and I did the worst thing you could possibly do: I took to the Internet to research. Down the rabbit hole I went, quickly becoming entangled in a web of confusing sourdough lingo. Leaven builds? Baker's percentages? The more I dug around, the more I realized that there was a wealth of knowledge beyond my bubble, all of which was baffling yet intriguing at the same time.

Convinced that I could bake better bread, I ditched my original formula and came up with a new one. It was more technical and involved, and it seemed like the right way to make sourdough. But in reality, it had quite the opposite effect. My once-beautiful, crispy crust was now tough and leathery, and the inside crumb left much to be desired. Looking back, there was nothing wrong with implementing a new technique, except for the itty-bitty fact that I relied way too heavily on instruction and lost touch with the art.

And so, after several failed loaves, I just gave up. Sourdough took a back seat, and I started tempering and eating dark chocolate instead. However, during my hiatus, I never stopped thinking about sourdough. I published a tutorial on my blog called "Sourdough Bread: A Beginner's Guide" because at the time, a go-to guide did not exist. Everything seemed far too advanced, and there just wasn't enough for the beginner. This was my attempt to bridge the gap and to help others in a way that was easier to understand. As a result, it created an online hub connecting people all over the world looking for the same thing. And to this day, it has become the most popular post on my blog.

What I've come to realize, hundreds of loaves later, is that sourdough is not paint-by-numbers; it's a blend of personal expression and technique. It's also community, sharing, wonderment, and, ultimately, an ongoing journey that has brought me to the pages of this book. Whether you're in it for the science or just a slice, baking bread is one of the most rewarding things you can do. And now, I'm excited to share that journey with you.

This book offers an inspired, simplified approach to making sourdough at home, based on my experience. It also provides the knowledge you'll need, all in one spot, to expand your horizons so you don't fall down the rabbit hole like I did. Just remember, the secret to your success doesn't lie within the formula itself. It's about unlocking your inner potential, trusting your intuition, and learning from your mistakes. My hope is that this book does for you what Celia did for me, and inspires you to begin and share your own sourdough journey.

ABOUT THE INGREDIENTS

The beauty of sourdough is that you only need a few simple ingredients to create nourishing bread at home. You will be amazed, time and time again, by how easy it is to transform the ordinary to the extraordinary right in your very own kitchen.

FLOUR

When I first started with sourdough, all white flours looked the same to me. I only knew the difference between bleached and unbleached flour. What I didn't realize was that protein content, wheat variety, and overall freshness mattered. This is why you'll get different results with different brands, which took me ages to figure out. But it doesn't mean you need to get fancy or buy the most expensive brand of flour on the market.

For the best results, simply choose a good-quality flour that's unbleached and does not contain any chemical additives. I'll never forget: I accidentally fed my starter with old cake flour for several days, which is essentially bleached flour (among other things), and it wouldn't rise at all. Also, make sure to check the expiration date. You'd be surprised at how many expired bags of flour sit on the shelves.

Nowadays, you can easily find a wide variety of good-quality flours in grocery stores and online. Bread flour is most commonly used by bread bakers, for its high gluten and protein content. It creates a strong dough, giving better structure and overall height to your bread. It also promotes a more chewy texture.

Comparatively speaking, all-purpose flour contains less gluten and absorbs less water, and it can still be used in some breads. You'll find that it creates a more light and fluffy texture in the finished loaf. So, you might be wondering: Can bread flour and all-purpose flour be used interchangeably? In some cases, absolutely. For example, both flours can be used to feed your sourdough starter. For baking, however, results will vary depending on the type of bread you're looking to create. Want soft and fluffy focaccia? Try all-purpose flour. Want bread with a lofty rise? Try bread flour. I like to blend flours to create interesting and unique textures.

Finally, whole-grain flours, which you'll learn more about later on, contain more minerals than white flours, which speed up fermentation in both your sourdough starter and the rise of your dough. These flours are typically more "thirsty" and require additional water when mixing.

The bottom line is that not all flour is created equal. As you continue to bake, you'll find your preference with practice, and it's certainly fun to experiment. My go-to is King Arthur Flour for reputable quality, taste, and performance.

WATER

There is great debate among the baking community with regard to water quality. Some say tap water is perfectly fine to use in sourdough baking and to feed your starter. Others strongly advise against this, due to the presence of chemicals and chlorine that can alter the strength of your yeast. Because water quality varies, you will have to be the judge on this one. It's best to use filtered or purified water when possible, for more consistent results.

SALT

I use La Baleine fine-grain sea salt for my sourdough. The small granules dissolve easily, and the flavor is bright. Salt not only adds flavor, but it also naturally preserves your bread. If you prefer to use a different salt for the sourdough recipes in this book, feel free to experiment with the quantities to your liking.

SOURDOUGH STARTER

In sourdough baking, a live fermented culture of flour and water is used in place of common commercial yeast. Within this culture, naturally occuring wild yeasts found on the grains of wheat mingle with friendly bacteria. Once bubbly and active, only a small portion is needed to make your bread rise. Whether you've created your own sourdough starter from scratch or it was a gift from a friend, strong and vibrant starters are essential to sourdough bread.

ABOUT THE TOOLS

Certain tools make life easier in the kitchen, and with sourdough, there's no exception. Here are your four must-have basics for baking better bread.

THE POT AND PARCHMENT PAPER

Steam is essential to bread. Without it, the dough might form a crust too quickly, leading to dense and heavy loaves. When I first started with sourdough, my loaves would rip and tear on the sides, and I couldn't figure out why. Baking in covered pots is a practical solution and is a common steaming technique used at home. Not all breads require a pot. But for large, crusty loaves, this is the best way to go for consistent results.

Any oven-safe pot will do, including a Dutch oven, deep casserole dish, or even a pizza stone with an inverted bowl. Another option is the enamel roaster, a brilliant tip from my friend Celia. Enamel roasters are lightweight, easy to store, and inexpensive—you can find them online, round and oval, for under $20.

Regarding pot size, the bigger, the better in my opinion. This allows for increased air circulation for even baking. But slightly smaller sizes will work, too. Just make sure that your pot, including the handles and lid, are oven-safe up to 450–500°F (230–260°C).

- Oval pot: 6¾ quarts (6.4 L) or 16 inches (40 cm)
- Round pot: 5½ quarts (5.2 L) or 10¼ inches (26 cm)

To prevent the dough from sticking, use non-stick parchment paper to line the pot. It is more reliable than flour or cornmeal and can be reused when in good condition.

THE SCALE

Weighing your ingredients is a tough sell, especially when you are accustomed to measuring in volume. Even in culinary school, where we worked exclusively in metrics, my trusty old measuring cups were still used at home. It wasn't until I became a bread baker that I finally realized the value. Allow me to explain.

Weight and volume measurements are not equivalents. They're only approximate. For example, if both you and I were to measure one cup of flour and then weigh it, we'd get a range of weights, based on how the flour was packed. Some of us lightly fluff our flour and sweep off the excess, while others pack it down like brown sugar. There's a difference. The scale on the other hand, tells you like it is (just like weighing yourself).

So why does this matter? Does everything have to be exact? As you continue to bake, you'll notice that bread dough is like a chameleon. Take one dough, add more water to it, and it becomes something entirely new. That's just the nature of bread. Weighing your ingredients, including all liquids, gives you more control over your results without the guesswork. For convenience, I've included both metric and volume measurements. However, since I *strongly* encourage you to weigh your ingredients, the weights are listed first in the bread recipes as a friendly reminder.

How to Weigh Your Ingredients

To use a digital kitchen scale, place an empty bowl onto the scale and press the "zero" or "tare" button to clear the weight. Then add your first ingredient to the bowl. Press the zero button to clear the weight once more, and repeat this process until you have weighed all of your ingredients. This all-in-one-bowl technique eliminates the need to weigh each ingredient separately and is speedy, effective, and minimizes clean-up.

THE BENCH SCRAPER

This one is my favorite. The bench scraper is to bakers as a spatula is to pancakes. You'll want this convenient extra hand when trying to move, shape, and transfer the dough, especially if it's sticky. You can find a bench scraper online or at any kitchen store.

HOW TO CREATE A SOURDOUGH STARTER

Creating a starter from scratch is very simple to do and ultimately marks the beginning of an ongoing relationship. It's also the most intimidating part of the sourdough baking process because it's often misunderstood. In this section, you'll get a crash course on sourdough starters from A to Z. You'll begin by making your own homemade culture, and you'll learn how to keep it bubbly and active with storage options and tips. You'll also learn how to care for your starter and keep it alive, to use for the recipes in this book and beyond. And because sourdough is meant to be shared, you'll also learn how to carry on the tradition with family and friends.

SOURDOUGH STARTER STEP-BY-STEP

Sourdough starters can be made a few different ways, with methods that include fruit juices, grapes, honey, and even potatoes to boost natural fermentation. In my experience, all you need are two simple ingredients: flour and water. Once combined, the culture will begin to ferment, developing the wild yeasts and bacteria needed to make your bread rise.

When creating a sourdough starter, it's important to begin with whole-grain flour to jumpstart the fermentation process. Whole wheat, rye, and spelt flour are great choices. Temperature and location also play important roles, so for best results, find a warm spot for your starter to thrive. My starter lives in a cozy cabinet right next to the fridge.

What to expect: The overall process will take about seven days from start to finish. My best advice is to be flexible with timing because developing yeast can be unpredictable. Your starter is ready when it has doubled in size, with plenty of bubbles on the surface and throughout the culture.

DAY 1: Add 60 grams (½ cup) of whole wheat flour and 60 grams (¼ cup) of water to a large jar. Mix with a fork to combine; the consistency will be thick and pasty. If measuring by volume, add more water to thin out the texture. Cover loosely with plastic wrap or a small cloth, and let it rest in a warm spot for 24 hours. (See photo #1, page 17.)

DAY 2: Check to see whether any bubbles, which may look like small black dots, have appeared on the surface. Bubbles indicate fermentation. It's okay if you don't see anything, as the bubbles might have appeared and dissolved overnight while you were sleeping. Rest the starter for another 24 hours. (See photo #2, page 17.)

DAY 3: Whether bubbles are visible or not, it's time to start the feeding process. To begin, remove and discard approximately half of your starter from the jar. The texture will be very stretchy. Add 60 grams (½ cup) of all-purpose flour and 60 grams (¼ cup) of water. Mix with a fork until smooth. (See photo #3, page 17.) The texture should resemble thick batter or plain yogurt at this point, so add more water as needed. Cover loosely, and let rest for another 24 hours.

DAYS 4, 5, AND 6: Repeat the feeding process outlined on Day 3. As the yeast begins to develop, your starter will rise, and bubbles will form on the surface and throughout the culture. (See photo #5, page 17.) When the starter falls, it's time to feed it again. *Tip:* Place a rubber band or piece of masking tape around the jar to measure the starter's growth as it rises.

DAY 7: By now, you should see plenty of bubbles, both large and small. The texture will be spongy and puffy, similar to roasted marshmallows. (See photo #6 above.) Take in the aroma. It should smell pleasant and not astringent. If these conditions are met, your starter is now active and ready to use. *Tip:* If your starter is not ready at this point, which is quite common, continue the feeding process for one to two weeks or more.

The very last step is to transfer your starter to a nice, clean jar. In keeping with tradition, you can also name it. My starter is called Dillon, after my oldest boy.

GOOD TO KNOW: HOOCH

During the creation process, and even after your starter has been established, you may notice a dark residual liquid on the surface or throughout the culture. It has a very distinctive smell, similar to rubbing alcohol or gym socks. This liquid is called "hooch" and is an indication that your starter needs to be fed. Any time you see this liquid, it's best to remove it (if possible) along with any discolored starter present. Some bakers choose to stir this liquid back into their starter, which can add a more sour flavor to the dough. However, in my opinion, hooch is wasted energy and is not always ideal to use. (Photo #4 above shows a layer of hooch in a starter.)

HOW TO CARE FOR YOUR SOURDOUGH STARTER

So you've created a sourdough starter. Now what?! Just like any living creature, it must be kept alive and well with regular feeds to maintain its strength. If your starter is not strong, your bread will not rise. Caring for your starter is easier than you'd think, and it certainly won't take hours of your time. I assure you: Feeding a teenage human is much scarier.

This section is chock full of information and is here for your reference to gain a better understanding without the guesswork. It's not required reading before making your first loaf of sourdough. However, the way you care for your starter now and in the future will directly impact the look, taste, and feel of your bread.

Feeding Your Starter

As you've done in the previous section, begin by removing and discarding about half of your starter. Replenish what's left in the jar with fresh flour and water. Cover loosely, and let it rise at room temperature until bubbly and double in size. Once it falls, the bubbles will become frothy and eventually disappear. Then you'll know it's time to feed your starter again.

What Kind of Flour Should Be Used?

As a rule of thumb, it's best to feed your starter with the same flour it's made of. When you created your starter, whole wheat flour was used to initially jumpstart the fermentation process. Then, it was fed all-purpose flour to foster healthy and balanced bacteria within the culture. You'll want to continue feeding your starter with all-purpose flour for optimal results. However, if you run out, you can also use bread flour.

How Much Flour and Water Does It Need to Be Fed?

Just like humans, your starter will require different amounts of food on different days. In general, feed your starter with equal parts of flour and water by weight, also known as 100% hydration. This is the most common type of sourdough starter and is characterized by a thick, batter-like texture.

However, if you're wondering about an approximate quantity of flour and water, follow a 1:1:1 feeding ratio as your guide. For example, if you have 60 grams (½ cup) of starter in the jar, feed it with 60 grams (½ cup) of flour and 60 grams (¼ cup) of water. In my experience, this feeding ratio will keep your starter well-fed and happy. If you're lucky, it will stay fully risen for quite a while before it begins to collapse.

By the way, there's a common myth that if your starter is left unfed and forgotten, it will stop working and die. And in some cases, sure, this can happen. But sourdough starters are much more resilient than you'd think. They're like house plants; on some days they will look vibrant and strong, and on other days they will look unsightly. The key is to find balance. Feed your starter in the morning while you're making coffee or at night before you go to bed. It will only take a minute. Eventually, you'll fall into an effortless routine, and feeding your starter will just become second nature.

When Is Your Starter Ready to Use?

After feeding, your starter is ready when it shows all of the following signs:

- Bulk growth to about double in size
- Small and large bubbles on the surface and throughout the culture
- Spongy or fluffy texture
- Pleasant aroma (not reminiscent of nail polish remover/gym socks/rubbing alcohol)

If you're having trouble spotting the signs, don't forget to place a rubber band around the base of the jar to measure the starter's growth. You can also try the float test, a helpful trick I learned from Chad Robertson's *Tartine Bread*. Drop a small dollop of starter into a glass of water. If it floats to the top, it's ready to use. Your starter can take anywhere from two to eight hours to become active.

How to Use Your Starter

To use your starter in a recipe, spoon or pour a portion from the jar to weigh or measure. Some bakers prefer to stir down their starter first, but I pour mine directly from the jar. Any time you use your starter, don't forget to replenish the jar with another feed, which is indicated in the recipes as a reminder.

Storage Options

Once your starter is established, you have two storage options to consider.

Room Temperature: If you bake often—let's say a few times a week—store your starter at room temperature. This will speed up fermentation, making the starter bubbly, active, and ready to use faster. Room temperature starters should be fed one to two times a day, depending on how quickly they rise and fall.

In the Fridge: If you don't bake that often, store your starter in the fridge, loosely covered or with a lid. You'll only need to feed it about once a week or so, to maintain its strength when not in use. There's no need to warm it up before feeding or to leave it at room temperature afterwards. Just give it a feed and pop it back into the fridge. However, when you are ready to make dough, feed your starter at room temperature as needed, to wake it back up.

Dried Starters (for you, and to share with friends)

So here's an interesting story.

One morning, I heard a strange hissing sound coming from the kitchen. I didn't think much of it, and I went about my business. Then, I heard the hissing sound again. And again. Turns out, it was coming from my sourdough starter. It had reached the top of the jar and was about to burst through the lid. But I became distracted (kids) and left my jar to fend for itself. The starter actually blew out through the *bottom* of the jar, breaking right through the glass! I watched helplessly as my precious bubbly friend puddled on the counter, eventually dripping all over the floor. It was finished.

Every now and then, I'll dry out my starter to retrieve for moments like this. It's like insurance. Drying your starter is not only a convenient back-up plan, it's also the easiest way to share it with family and friends. Whether it's hand-delivered or mailed overseas, the recipient can begin their journey whenever they want. That's how I got started.

How to Dry Your Sourdough Starter

Once your starter is bubbly and active, line a rimmed sheet pan with parchment paper or a nonstick silicone mat. Spread a thin layer of starter on top, smoothing it out with the back of a spoon. Let it air dry in the oven (turned off) until the texture becomes crispy. This can take anywhere from two to three days or more. Once it is completely dry, break the starter into small pieces. Store in a ziptop bag in a cool spot, such as a cabinet, drawer, or pantry. It should last for at least six months, possibly up to one year.

To Reactivate Your Dried Starter

STEP 1: In the morning, add 15 grams (1 tbsp) of dried starter, 30 grams (¼ cup) of all-purpose flour, and 30 grams (2 tbsp) of water into a large jar. Mix well, cover loosely, and let rest at room temperature.

STEP 2: In the afternoon, add 30 grams (¼ cup) of all-purpose flour and 30 grams (2 tbsp) of water to the jar. Mix well and let rest.

STEP 3: In the evening, add 60 grams (½ cup) of all-purpose flour and 60 grams (¼ cup) of water. Mix well and let rest overnight. In the morning, remove and discard about half of your starter and repeat step 2 until it has doubled in size.

Sourdough Starter FAQ

1. My starter is taking a long time to rise. Why?

This can happen at any time—when creating a starter or after it has been established. First, find a warm spot where your starter can thrive. Wrap a warm towel around the jar, put it under a desk lamp, or even place it near a heater to speed things up. You can also try using warm water in your feeds. Another issue could be your flour. For best results, always use unbleached flour.

2. Can I use commercial yeast to make my starter rise faster?

Commercial yeast will make your starter and bread dough rise faster. However, this is not true sourdough. It's technically a hybrid.

3. Can I make an all-spelt or all-rye flour starter?

Spelt and rye starters are typically successful because of their high mineral content. However, these flours are more expensive than other flours. Because you will remove a portion of your starter before feeding, this might not be a practical option.

4. Why do I have to remove and discard a portion of the starter?

This is the most common question I receive about the feeding process. First, the exact amount you remove is not set in stone. Some days it might be more or less, depending on the condition of your starter, what it looks like, and what it smells like. I recommend removing at least half, which is fairly easy to judge by eye. Doing so will rebalance the acidity levels within the culture, which produces a mild sour flavor.

Second, if you didn't remove some of your starter, guess how much you'd end up with? Removing some reduces the total amount to smaller, more practical proportions, making it easier to manage. The good news is that, in most cases, you can save leftover starter to use in recipes other than bread. For that reason, I've included a whole chapter on this. See page 147 for creative ideas.

5. Once my starter doubles in size, or peaks, what is the window of time for using it for a recipe?

It all depends on the nature of your starter. Some days, it will rise and fall so quickly it will leave you baffled. Other days, it will stay peaked for several hours. If you feed your starter following the 1:1:1 ratio and get to know its temperament, then your window of time will be easier to judge. I recommend using peaked starter as soon as possible, preferably within the hour, before it falls.

6. How do I know if I have enough starter for my recipes?

The recipes in this book require anywhere from 50 grams (¼ cup) to 250 grams (1¼ cups). You can easily adjust the amount following the instructions in the next question.

7. How can I increase the total amount of my starter?

First, transfer your starter into a bigger jar, if necessary. Give it a feed, and wait for it to become bubbly and active. Before it falls, give it another feed without removing half of it first. Repeat this technique until you have reached your desired amount.

8. I'm going away on vacation. Is my starter going to die?

Don't worry. You don't need a babysitter. Feed your starter and pop it directly in the fridge. It will continue to rise, and you might even see bubbles. But eventually, it will go dormant. After you return, don't be surprised if it takes a few days to revive. Feed your starter at room temperature as needed to wake it back up.

9. How can I revive a neglected starter?

It's possible that your starter might get pushed to the back of the fridge, only to be lost behind the Chinese takeout containers for months on end. It might look gray and discolored and smell very potent. But don't give up hope! Discard most of your starter and transfer what you keep into a new, clean jar. Feed it for several days at room temperature in a warm spot. Be patient and consistent, as it might take one to two weeks to revive. If you're unsuccessful, create a new starter. And if you ever see mold, throw all of it out and start again.

10. I already have my own sourdough starter. Can I use it for your recipes?

The recipes in this book have been tested with a 100% hydration starter. If you're using a different type of starter, your results may vary, but only slightly. It certainly doesn't hurt to experiment.

11. What is a leaven or levain?

Oftentimes, you'll hear the terms "leaven" and "sourdough starter" used interchangeably. Simply put: Your starter is the mothership and your leaven is an offshoot. Leavens are typically fed with different types of flour to build specific flavor profiles without changing the integrity of the original starter. For example, if you pour some of your starter into a bowl and feed it with rye flour, you've just created a leaven. Your original jar of sourdough starter, fed exclusively with all-purpose flour, remains untouched. There are many benefits to this technique in terms of building flavor. However, it takes more time—typically overnight—and I have not used it in this book. "Levain" is the French term for leaven.

BAKING YOUR FIRST LOAF
A Starting Point and Beyond

Once your starter is bubbly and your essential tools are ready to go, so are you. In this chapter, you'll find two sourdough staples. My Everyday Sourdough (page 26) is a fantastic introduction for the beginner, with minimal effort required. When you're ready for more of a challenge, come back to this chapter and try baking my High-Hydration Sourdough (page 29) for comparison. Understanding the similarities and differences between the two loaves will show you how to fit slow bread into any modern schedule and create the style of sourdough that you want.

With that said, don't worry about understanding all of the details and techniques right away. Just jump right in and have fun. When curiosity kicks in—and it will—refer to the more detailed information at the end of the chapter at your leisure. That way, you won't fall down the rabbit hole like I did.

EVERYDAY SOURDOUGH

Makes 1 Loaf

Every baker needs an all-purpose, go-to loaf in their repertoire. And if you're new to sourdough, this is the perfect place to start. Simply make the dough, let it rise overnight, and bake in the morning. It requires very little effort with big reward. The crust is golden and crunchy, and the velvety crumb is perfect for sandwiches and toast. Try a few thick-cut slices with creamy avocado and tomato or the most delicious grilled cheese sandwich you will ever sink your teeth into. This is my family's favorite loaf.

About the Dough: Because this dough rises while you're asleep, you won't be tempted to rush the process or check on it every five seconds to see if it's ready. Have a look at the baker's schedule, then make adjustments to suit your own schedule. The overnight method can be applied to most of the recipes in this book.

BAKER'S SCHEDULE

Thursday–Saturday: Feed your starter until bubbly and active.

Saturday Evening: Make the dough, and let rise overnight.

Sunday Morning: Shape the dough, let rise again, score, and bake.

50 g (¼ cup) bubbly, active starter

350 g (1⅓ cups plus 2 tbsp) warm water

500 g (4 cups plus 2 tbsp) bread flour

9 g (1½ tsp) fine sea salt

MAKE THE DOUGH: In the evening, whisk the starter and water together in a large bowl with a fork. Add the flour and salt. Combine until a stiff dough forms, then finish mixing by hand to fully incorporate the flour. The dough will feel dense and shaggy, and it will stick to your fingers as you go. Scrape off as much as you can. Cover with a damp towel and let rest for 30 minutes. Replenish your starter with fresh flour and water, and store according to preference.

After the dough has rested, work the mass into a fairly smooth ball. To do this, grab a portion of the dough and fold it over, pressing your fingertips into the center. Repeat, working your way around the dough until it begins to tighten, about 15 seconds.

BULK RISE: Cover the bowl with a damp towel and let rise overnight at room temperature. This will take about 8 to 10 hours at 70°F (21°C). The dough is ready when it no longer looks dense and has doubled in size.

SHAPE: In the morning, coax the dough onto a lightly floured work surface. To shape it into a round, start at the top and fold the dough over toward the center. Turn the dough slightly and fold over the next section of dough. Repeat until you have come full circle. Flip the dough over and let rest for 5 to 10 minutes. Meanwhile, line an 8-inch (20-cm) bowl with a towel and dust with flour. With floured hands, gently cup the dough and pull it toward you in a circular motion to tighten its shape. Using a bench scraper, place the dough into the bowl, seam side up.

SECOND RISE: Cover the bowl and let rest for 30 minutes to 1 hour. The dough is ready when it looks puffy and has risen slightly but has not yet doubled in size.

Preheat your oven to 450°F (230°C). Cut a sheet of parchment paper to fit the size of your baking pot, leaving enough excess around the sides to remove the bread.

SCORE: Place the parchment over the dough and invert the bowl to release. Sprinkle the dough with flour and gently rub the surface with your hands. Using the tip of a small, serrated knife or a razor blade, score the dough with the cross-cut pattern on page 195, or any way you'd like. Use the parchment to transfer the dough to the baking pot.

BAKE: Bake the dough on the center rack for 20 minutes, covered. Remove the lid, and continue to bake for 30 minutes. Then, carefully remove the loaf from the pot and bake directly on the oven rack for the last 10 minutes to crisp the crust. When finished, transfer to a wire rack. Cool for 1 hour before slicing.

Sourdough is best consumed on the same day it is baked. To maximize freshness, cool completely and store at room temperature in a plastic bag for up to 1 day.

HIGH-HYDRATION SOURDOUGH

Makes 1 Loaf

Just scour over any bread forum and you'll see that everyone wants to know the same thing: How do you bake sourdough with big, open holes? I'll be honest: The answer is not black and white. A perfect storm of variables, including a bit of luck, has often dubbed this sourdough the "Holy Grail." So why bother, you ask? Well, it's all part of the charm. Because once you've discovered this incredible loaf, you'll be eager to devour it on the spot.

About the Dough: The first step toward bigger holes is to add more water, or to increase the dough's hydration. The second step is to expand your sourdough technique: Gently dimple the dough after the bulk rise (think: focaccia) and then shape it twice. Both techniques will help to open up the crumb and can be applied toward other doughs to achieve the same effect. If you're working with King Arthur bread flour, which is a high-gluten flour, you can replace up to 60 grams (½ cup) with all-purpose flour to lighten the texture.

BAKER'S SCHEDULE

Thursday and Friday: Feed your starter until bubbly and active.

Saturday Evening: Make the dough and let rise overnight.

Sunday Morning: Shape the dough, let rise again, score, and bake.

50 g (¼ cup) bubbly, active starter
375 g (1½ cups plus 1 tbsp) warm water
500 g (4 cups plus 2 tbsp) bread flour
9 g (1½ tsp) fine sea salt

NOTE: In baker's terms, hydration is the total amount of water (or liquid) divided by the total amount of flour. This dough is considered high hydration at 75% and is a wet dough. Low-hydration doughs, which are drier and have smaller holes, fall in the 50% to 68% range.

MAKE THE DOUGH: In the evening, whisk the starter and water together in a large bowl with a fork. Add the flour and salt. Mix to combine, then finish by hand to form a rough dough. Cover with a damp towel and let rest for 1 hour. Replenish your starter with fresh flour and water, and store according to preference. After the dough has rested, work it into a ball, about 15 to 20 seconds.

BULK RISE: Cover the bowl with a damp towel and let rise overnight at room temperature, about 8 to 10 hours at 70°F (21°C). The dough is ready when it has doubled in size, has a few bubbles on the surface, and jiggles when you move the bowl from side to side.

SHAPE: In the morning, coax the dough onto a floured surface. Dimple the dough all over with floured fingertips. Gently shape it into a round and let rest for 5 to 10 minutes. Meanwhile, line an 8-inch (20-cm) bowl or proofing basket with a towel and dust with flour. Using a bench scraper, scoop up the dough and flip it over so that the smooth side is facing down. Shape it again, and then flip it back over. Cup the dough and gently pull it toward you in a circular motion to tighten its shape. Place into your lined bowl, seam side up.

SECOND RISE: Cover the dough and refrigerate for 1 hour to set its structure. Note: You can chill this dough for up to 6 hours or more. When ready to bake, let sit at room temperature while the oven heats up.

Preheat your oven to 500°F (260°C). Cut a piece of parchment to fit the size of your baking pot.

SCORE: Place the parchment over the dough and invert the bowl to release. Dust the surface with flour and rub with your hands to coat. Using the tip of a small knife or a razor blade, score the dough with the bird wings pattern on page 195, or any way you'd like. Use the parchment to transfer the dough into the baking pot.

BAKE: Place the pot on the center rack, and reduce the heat to 450°F (230°C). Bake the dough for 20 minutes, covered. Remove the lid, and continue to bake for 30 minutes. Lift the loaf out of the pot, and bake directly on the oven rack for the last 10 minutes. Cool on a wire rack for 1 hour before slicing.

This loaf will stay fresh up to 1 day stored at room temperature in a plastic bag.

SOURDOUGH STEPS AT A GLANCE

Before you begin:
Feed your starter
until bubbly
and active.

Make the dough.

Let the dough rise.

Shape the dough.

Let the dough
rise again.

Score the dough.

Bake.

Cool, slice, and enjoy!

SOURDOUGH STEPS, EXPLAINED

As you continue to bake, you'll learn that sourdough is not just a recipe; it's an understanding. And because methods and terminology will vary from baker to baker, this can either intrigue or overwhelm. Here, I've broken down the basic steps, based on my experience with sourdough. Just like the previous chapter, this section is not required reading. Use this guide as a reference throughout the book, and to satisfy the curious mind.

Step 1: Make the Dough

The mixing process is pretty straightforward. Whether you do it by hand or with a stand mixer, the goal is to fully incorporate the ingredients. No one wants a chunk of flour or a salt patch in their bread. Unlike baking a cake, these lumps do not sort themselves out in the oven. Once fully incorporated, the dough will be rough, shaggy, sticky, and dense—all normal.

First Rest

After mixing, the dough needs to rest in the bowl. Resting is a repeated step throughout sourdough and is not worth rushing, as each rest serves a significant purpose.

Here, the flour needs time to absorb the water, which jumpstarts the gluten development without kneading. It also makes the dough more soft and manageable. Timing can be flexible depending on your schedule and the type of dough. For example, the Everyday Sourdough (page 26) does well with a 30-minute rest, whereas the High-Hydration Sourdough (page 29) and most whole-grain doughs could go for a full hour. Fillings, such as nuts and raisins, would be added after this resting period, because they will be easier to incorporate.

GOOD TO KNOW: AUTOLYZE

The technical term for this first rest is "autolyze." A true autolyze does not contain salt or yeast, as some bakers believe that these ingredients prohibit gluten development. From an everyday perspective, my all-in-one-bowl method works just fine. However, it's technically a hybrid autolyze, which is worth noting for comparison when you encounter this term.

Quick Knead

Once the dough has completed the first rest, give it a quick knead in the bowl. The idea is to work the dough, folding it over several times, pressing your fingertips into the center as you go. Don't worry about technique here. Just keep moving the dough around until the gluten begins to tighten, which will indicate that it's time to stop. That's your signal. This can take anywhere from 15 seconds to 1 minute, depending on the dough.

By the way, please don't be put off by the word "knead." Gone are the days of old ladies with forearms the size of turkey legs pounding bread dough until the cows come home. There are many ways to knead, and this step is minimal at best. Sadly, the stigma still remains, which is why kneading is often misunderstood. This quick movement not only incorporates air into the dough to further develop the gluten, it's also your last chance to adjust the dough. If it's too sticky, or if you find a few dry bits of flour at the bottom of the bowl, get in there and fix it. Consider it quality control.

Combine the ingredients to form a rough and shaggy dough. Let rest for 30 minutes to 1 hour.

Work the dough into a ball (A).

Work the dough into a ball (B).

Let rise until the dough is double in size.

Step 2: Bulk Rise

Now, it's time for the dough to rise.

The first thing I should mention is that sourdough needs to rise twice. The bulk rise, otherwise known as the first rise or bulk fermentation, is when most of the gluten development takes place. "Gluten" refers to the protein strands found in wheat, essential for overall structure and height. Rush the bulk rise, and you'll end up with a brick so flat the squirrels won't even touch it.

How Long Does It Take?

Sourdough will never be ready in one hour, and unlike commercial yeasted breads, you don't want it to be. Embrace the pace, and you'll be rewarded with the most delicious, complex flavor. Time also allows for natural fermentation, which breaks down the nutrition inhibitors associated with wheat. As an added bonus, a long and slow rise conveniently works around a busy day—whether at home or in the office—so you can go about your business and stop hovering over the bowl.

For a general timeframe, temperature plays a key role during the bulk rise. The doughs in this book can take anywhere from 6 to 10 or more hours to rise at room temperature, about 70°F (21°C). This is your benchmark. Obviously, it might be warmer or colder in your house, which is normal and explains why rise times are only approximate. If I could say this one hundred times, I would. Don't be surprised if your dough takes only five hours to rise in the summer, but maybe twelve hours in winter. When this happens, just go with it. Use your intuition and senses to judge when the dough is ready. As bakers will often say, "Watch the dough, not the clock."

GOOD TO KNOW: WATER TEMPERATURE

Water temperature plays a significant role in rise times because it changes the temperature of your dough. Warm water, about 80°F (27°C), boosts the rise, and cooler water, about 70°F (21°C), slows it down. Knowing when and how to adjust water temperature is a helpful technique that can be tailored to suit your baking schedule, especially as the seasons change. For example, in the summer, I typically make my overnight doughs at around 9 or 10 PM with cool water to control the rise. By 6 AM, the dough is ready to go.

How Will I Know When the Dough Is Ready?

Not all doughs look the same when the bulk rise is complete, but many share the same characteristics.

Here are a few key signs to look for:

- An increase in growth, about double in size
- Dough no longer looks dense but rather is soft and pillowy
- Plenty of bubbles throughout the dough to show aeration
- A few bubbles on the surface, typical of wet and whole-grain doughs

GOOD TO KNOW: DOUBLE IN SIZE

Dough rises up and out to the sides, depending on its container. For example, if your bowl is large and wide and looks like it could feed salad for 30, then it will be hard for you to judge when the dough has doubled in size. Consider using a smaller mixing bowl, about 8 inches (20 cm) wide, or rising the dough in a tall, clear container with measuring marks. This way you'll know exactly how much the dough has grown.

Stretch and Folds

This is a minimal-kneading technique that gently incorporates air into the dough, adding strength and height to the finished loaf. For many bakers, it's an enjoyable process (who doesn't like to touch bread dough?) and can be applied as an optional step.

Stretch and folds are completed in sets. The first set can be done about 30 minutes into the bulk rise. Then, you'll complete up to 4 additional sets spaced 15 minutes to 1 hour apart, depending on the dough. This technique is very flexible; if you only have time for 1 or 2 sets, just go for it. You'll get excellent results either way. For photos illustrating these steps, see page 194.

Step 3: Shape

After the bulk rise, the dough is ready to be shaped on your work surface.

But first, let's talk about how to get the dough out of the bowl. Pull it? Stretch it? Dump it? I like to gently coax the dough out of the bowl, taking care not to deflate all of the air bubbles. It's best to do this with floured fingertips. Some bakers use a lightly oiled bowl to prevent sticking, but if you choose to stretch and fold the dough, you'll notice that it barely sticks to the bowl at all.

For shaping, follow the step-by-step instructions on pages 188 to 194 to get a basic idea of the process. Every baker has their own method, but the goal is to redistribute the weight of the dough and to create a tight skin on the surface for a more uniform rise. When shaping, too much flour on your work surface will make the dough slide around; not enough flour and the dough will stick. Try to find a balance for best results.

Bench Rest

Right after the dough is shaped, it needs to rest again. This rest, also known as the bench rest, can last anywhere from 5 to 10 minutes, or more, depending on the dough. Sorry, no shortcuts here. As mentioned earlier, resting is a repeated step with an important purpose. Or think of it this way: Gluten is like a muscle. If it's too stiff, it won't stretch. How would you feel after 100 squats?

Tighten the Shape

During the bench rest, the dough will spread naturally as the gluten begins to relax. For most loaves you'll need to tighten the shape before proceeding to the next step. To do this, with floured hands, gently cup the dough and pull it toward you, or pull it around in a circular motion. The idea is for the dough to catch enough surface tension to essentially do the tightening for you. This is a very easy technique that will only take a few seconds to do. Then the dough is placed into a towel-lined bowl or proofing basket, seam side up. Use a bench scraper for easy transfer.

NOTE: For some doughs, especially wet doughs, the shape will continue to spread even after tightening. When this happens, flip the dough over and shape it again for better oven spring.

GOOD TO KNOW: THE TEA TOWEL TRICK

Since most of us will only bake one loaf at a time, maybe a few times a month, lack of repetition is a common hurdle. For this reason, take the opportunity to practice on a small tea towel, folding over the corners and sides to emulate the motions of shaping. It might sound silly, but it works. The idea dawned on me while folding laundry, and I use this trick to this day, especially when trying out a new shaping technique.

Shape the dough, flip it over, and let it rest for 5 to 10 minutes.

Gently cup the dough to tighten the shape.

Place the dough into a bowl or proofing basket, seam side up (A).

Place the dough into a bowl or proofing basket, seam side up (B).

Step 4: Second Rise

After shaping, the dough needs to rise again.

The second rise, also known as the final proof, allows the dough to build back strength after shaping. Remember, during shaping, your dough will lose air from the simple act of human touch. Give it some time, and you'll be rewarded with better volume, texture, and flavor.

How Long Does the Second Rise Take?

In my experience, the second rise is based on the length of the bulk rise. Using our earlier benchmark, at room temperature, the second rise can take anywhere from 30 minutes to 1 hour for round and oval-shaped loaves. If you're making sandwich bread, it can take 1 to 2 hours, or until the dough rises above the rim of the pan. So, the bottom line? The rise time will vary. Again, watch the dough and not the clock. That's the secret.

Proofing Baskets

For some doughs, bakers will use proofing baskets, also known as brotforms or bannetons, to contain their shapes during the second rise. They are essential for wet doughs, like the High-Hydration Sourdough (page 29), as it will spread out like a pancake otherwise. When left unlined and very well-floured, these baskets will leave a beautiful powdered imprint on the crust, giving your loaf an instant artisan touch. You can find proofing baskets online, in 10-or 12-inch (25- or 30-cm) oval and 8- or 9-inch (20-or 23-cm) round shapes.

HOW TO SEASON A NEW PROOFING BASKET

A word to the wise: If your proofing basket is brand new, it needs to be seasoned before using. Otherwise the dough will stick. You'll only need to do this once. To begin, lightly brush the bottom and sides with water. Then generously coat the inside with a handful of flour, turning the basket and tapping out the excess as you go. The inside should look completely white when you are finished. Leave it to dry for a few hours and the surface will set. To use your seasoned proofing basket, sprinkle heavily with flour, removing any excess, and place your dough inside, seam side up.

When Is the Dough Ready to Bake?

The dough is ready when it puffs up and no longer looks dense. That's the main sign to look for. It will rise somewhat during this stage, but it does not need to double in size. If this happens, the dough might exhaust its strength before baking and possibly deflate in the oven. Bakers call deflated or collapsed dough overproofed.

One of the easiest ways to judge the dough's readiness is to take a picture on your phone. How much did it rise? What does it look like now? You'd be surprised at how helpful this is. You can also gently poke the dough with your finger; if it springs back slowly, it's ready to bake. This poke test isn't 100% accurate, however, and leaves much room for interpretation. With practice, you'll just know when the dough is ready.

GOOD TO KNOW: RETARDING THE DOUGH

If life happens and you run out of time to bake, you can always chill the dough during the second rise. This is also known as retarding the dough. The dough will still rise when refrigerated, but at a slower pace, due to the colder temperature. This technique can buy you up to 8 hours of time or more, depending on the strength of the dough. It also deepens the flavor, and some bakers argue that it promotes bigger holes in the crumb.

Step 5: Score

When the second rise is complete and your oven is preheated, you can score the dough.

Scoring or slashing the dough prior to baking serves both functional and decorative purposes. It allows steam to escape and controls the direction in which the loaf opens up. There are no rules for scoring, and not every type of bread needs to be scored, but there are guidelines. Your technique can be as simple or artistic as you'd like.

Tools of the Trade

A small, serrated steak knife or sharp paring knife works really well for scoring bread dough. Some bakers also use a razor blade or bread lame, which is essentially a razor blade attached to a small handle. Choose what you feel most comfortable with. I started out with a small steak knife because that's what I had at home. As I began to experiment with more intricate scoring patterns, I switched to a blade for more control. Although admittedly, I felt like Edward Scissorhands during the first few tries!

When scoring, the length and depth of each cut will vary according the texture of the dough and specific pattern you are trying to create. If you're new to the process, start simple. Make one long cut down the length of the loaf, about ¼ inch (6.3 mm) in depth, using the tip of the blade as your guide. For more specific scoring patterns and techniques, see page 195 for inspiration.

PLAYDOUGH MAKES PERFECT

Achieving the perfect score is not something that happens overnight. Every baker experiences that moment of hesitation, hovering over the dough before making their first slash. Consider practicing on a ball of playdough, especially with more artisan-style designs, until you feel more confident.

Step 6: Bake

Baking times and temperatures will vary according to recipe, and of course, all ovens are different. For years, I baked in a busted 1965 oven that wouldn't stay closed, causing precious heat and steam to escape—the door was held shut with a latch! Using an oven thermometer was extremely helpful for accuracy and is strongly recommended if you're having issues with temperature control.

Round and oval-shaped loaves baked in covered pots typically follow the same pattern: 20 minutes covered for steam, 30 minutes uncovered for color, and 10 minutes baked directly on the center rack to crisp the crust. The last 10 minutes on the rack also circulates the air evenly and eliminates any ring around the loaf from a pot that's too snug.

GOOD TO KNOW: NO NEED TO PREHEAT THE POT

Many breads baked in covered pots require the pot to be preheated beforehand. You can skip that step. Although a preheated pot allows for the dough to expand on contact, you'll get comparable results, avoiding the inevitable wrist burns.

Invert the dough onto a piece of parchment paper and dust with flour.

Score the dough.

Transfer the dough into a baking pot.

Bake the dough and enjoy!

How Will I Know When the Bread is Fully Baked?

First, knock on the bottom of the loaf. If it sounds hollow, like a drum, it's usually cooked through. If it sounds muffled (knock on the sides for comparison), it might need more time. An additional 10 minutes or more is fine in bread baking. Again, it's not like baking a cake. In this case, turn the oven down or off completely and give your loaf a few more minutes on the rack.

Second, your loaf should feel relatively lightweight. This indicates that the dough was properly fermented and most of the moisture has been cooked out. This can be tricky to judge without a reference point, but a brick is a brick.

Third, and most reliable, take its temperature. For doughs made without milk, butter, and eggs, the internal temperature should read about 200 to 210°F (93 to 99°C). For enriched dough, the temperature should be about 190 to 200°F (88 to 93°C). Use a digital thermometer for an accurate read.

Cooling Down

It's best for sourdough to cool on a wire rack before slicing. Try to aim for at least one hour or so. Cut into it too soon, and the texture will be gummy and eventually dry out. As the bread cools, additional steam will escape through the loaf, which might soften the crust. You'll actually hear a crackling sound as this happens—music to your ears! To avoid temperature shock, you can always cool your loaf inside the oven, turned off, with the door ajar.

Slicing Bread

Believe it or not, I get a lot of emails about slicing bread. It's not that people don't know how to do it. I think all of our bread knives need to be sharpened! So, that's the first step. You can also position the loaf on its side, to avoid pushing down on the crust while you cut the bread into slices.

GOOD TO KNOW: HOW DO YOU MAKE YOUR BREAD TASTE SOUR?

Not all sourdoughs will taste sour. Achieving this particular flavor depends on a number of factors, including how you care for your starter, flour type, temperature, and how the dough was fermented. And sometimes, it's a combination of these factors. For example, if you don't feed your starter that often, it will become more acidic and smell like vinegar, which adds more tang to your bread. The addition of whole-grain flour helps to achieve the same effect, as does chilling the dough overnight after it has been shaped. Finding the right flavor for your sourdough is something to experiment with and is not necessarily set in stone.

Storing and Freezing Bread

To fully experience sourdough, enjoy your bread fresh! Some loaves can hold up for one to two days, but it all depends. Always store your bread at room temperature in a plastic bag or bread box, if you have one. I use long, reusable bread bags that twist closed, which you can find online (see the Source List, page 196). Whatever you do, avoid chilling your bread, as it will become rubbery and might grow mold. Once completely cool, sourdough can be frozen whole or cut into slices. A layer of plastic wrap and foil should be sufficient for up to three months, or whenever freezer burn creeps in. Defrost at room temperature for best results.

SWEET *and* SAVORY ARTISAN LOAVES

An easy, creative way to enhance your sourdough is to fold different fillings and flavors into the dough. Imagine all of the possibilities: dried fruit soaked in vanilla extract and spices, rubbly bits of dark chocolate, and even fresh herbs and cheese. This was my favorite chapter to write, and admittedly, these are my favorite loaves to eat. The Decadent Chocolate Chip (page 42) is a great place to begin, or for something more savory, try the Dill and White Cheddar (page 45). Keep in mind that whatever flavors you choose to add will come through subtly in the finished loaves. (Chocolate sourdough does not taste like cake!)

DECADENT CHOCOLATE CHIP

Makes 1 Loaf

Reminiscent of the classic Pain au Chocolate, this sourdough is one of my favorites, hands down. The crumb, studded with rich chocolate chips, boasts a flavor and texture that's absolutely out of this world. The crust is baked dark and bold to provide extra crunch against the soft interior. Serve warm to experience the full-on decadence of sweet, melted chocolate in all its glory.

About the Dough: Due to the weight of the chocolate chips, this dough may take a bit longer than usual to rise, but be patient—it's worth it. When ready to score, the surface of the dough will be covered in chocolate chips; choose a scoring pattern that works around the chips to avoid a collision with your blade.

DOUGH

50 g (¼ cup) bubbly, active starter
375 g (1½ cups plus 1 tbsp) warm water
500 g (4 cups plus 2 tbsp) bread flour
9 g (1½ tsp) fine sea salt

FILLINGS

175 g (1 cup) semi-sweet chocolate chips

A few days before baking, feed your starter until bubbly and active. Store at room temperature until ready to use.

TIP: My kids love this sourdough with all kinds of chocolate—white, dark, milk—it's all good in our house. Feel free to experiment with your favorite combination.

MAKE THE DOUGH: In a large bowl, whisk the starter and water together with a fork. Add the flour and salt. Mix to combine, finishing by hand to fully incorporate the flour. Cover with a damp towel and let rest for 30 minutes. Replenish your starter with fresh flour and water, and store according to preference.

ADD THE FILLINGS: After the dough has rested, add the chocolate chips to the bowl. Gently knead them into the dough to incorporate, about 1 minute. Some of the chocolate chips will pop out as you go, which is okay.

BULK RISE: Cover the bowl with a damp towel and let rise at room temperature until double in size. This will take about 8 to 10 hours at 70°F (21°C).

SHAPE: Coax the dough onto a lightly floured work surface. Shape it into a round or oval and let rest for 5 to 10 minutes. Line an 8-inch (20-cm) bowl or 10-inch (24-cm) oval proofing basket with a towel and dust with flour. Cup the dough and gently tighten according to your desired shape. Place into your proofing vessel, seam side up.

SECOND RISE: Cover the dough and let rest until puffy but not fully risen, about 30 minutes to 1 hour, depending on temperature.

Preheat your oven to 500°F (260°C). Cut a sheet of parchment paper to fit the size of your baking pot.

SCORE: Place the parchment over the dough and invert the proofing vessel to release. Dust the dough with flour and rub it in gently to coat. Choose a scoring pattern from the ideas on page 195, or simply make one long cut down the length of the loaf. Use the parchment to transfer the dough into the baking pot.

BAKE: Place the dough onto the center rack, and reduce the heat to 450°F (230°C). Bake for 20 minutes, covered. Remove the lid, and continue to bake for 40 minutes. When finished, transfer the loaf to a wire rack and cool, about 1 hour, before slicing.

Once completely cool, store in a plastic bag at room temperature for up to 1 day.

DILL and WHITE CHEDDAR

Makes 1 Loaf

Cheddar and dill is a classic combination. In this recipe, the cheddar is grated, not cubed, so it melts seamlessly into the dough when baked. This brings out the tangy notes of sourdough, and when paired with fresh dill, the flavor will knock your socks off. Try a few slices toasted with a warm winter stew or zesty vegetarian chili.

About the Dough: This dough is sticky but well worth it, as the increased amount of water and gentle shaping helps to develop a more open crumb. To deepen the flavor and make it easier to score, the dough is chilled overnight after it has been shaped.

DOUGH
50 g (¼ cup) bubbly, active starter
400 g (1⅔ cups) warm water
500 g (4 cups plus 2 tbsp) bread flour
9 g (1½ tsp) fine sea salt

FILLINGS
10 g (3 tbsp) chopped fresh dill
100 g (1 cup) grated sharp white cheddar cheese

A few days before baking, feed your starter until bubbly and active. Store at room temperature until ready to use.

MAKE THE DOUGH: In the morning, whisk the starter and water together in a large bowl with a fork. Add the flour and salt. Mix to combine, finishing by hand until no lumps of flour remain. Cover with a damp towel and let rest for 1 hour. Replenish your starter with fresh flour and water, and store according to preference.

ADD THE FILLINGS: After the dough has rested, add the chopped dill and cheddar to the bowl. Gently knead the fillings into the dough to incorporate, about 1 minute. It will smell fantastic. Cover the bowl and let rest for 30 minutes.

BULK RISE WITH STRETCH AND FOLDS: With lightly wet hands, grab a portion of the dough, stretch it upward, and fold it over toward the center of the bowl. Give the bowl a one-quarter turn and repeat until you have come full circle to complete your first set. Repeat this technique, about 3 to 4 sets, spaced 15 minutes apart. See page 194 for more details.

Once your stretch and folds are complete, cover the dough with a damp towel and let rise at room temperature, 70°F (21°C), for about 8 to 10 hours. The dough is ready when it has doubled in size and has a few bubbles on the surface.

SHAPE: Coax the dough onto a lightly floured work surface. Shape it into a round or oval and let rest for 5 to 10 minutes. Line an 8-inch (20-cm) bowl or 10-inch (24-cm) oval proofing basket with a towel and dust with flour. Cup the dough and gently tighten according to your desired shape. Place into your proofing vessel, seam side up.

SECOND RISE: Cover the dough and transfer directly to the fridge. Chill overnight, up to 8 to 12 hours.

Preheat your oven to 500°F (260°C). Remove the dough from the fridge while the oven heats up. Cut a sheet of parchment paper to fit the size of your baking pot.

SCORE: Place the parchment over the dough and invert the proofing vessel to release. Dust the dough with flour and rub it in gently with your hands. Score the dough straight down the center, using the tip of a small knife or razor blade. Use the parchment to transfer the dough into the baking pot.

BAKE: Place the pot on the center rack, and reduce the heat to 450°F (230°C). Bake for 20 minutes, covered. Remove the lid, and continue to bake for 30 minutes. Lift the loaf out of the pot, and finish baking directly on the oven rack for the last 10 minutes. Cool for 1 hour before slicing.

This loaf will stay fresh up to 1 to 2 days stored at room temperature in a plastic bag.

OLIVE, THYME, and PARMESAN

Makes 1 Loaf

The aroma of this sourdough bread is incredible. Fragrant lemon zest, woodsy thyme, and briny olives—just close your eyes and imagine you're in the Mediterranean! For variety and color, I like to use a blend of mixed olives, including kalamatas, niçoise, and cerignolas, the plump red and green ones. You can easily find these olives in the deli section of your grocery store. The Parmesan, nutty and sweet, is sprinkled onto the crust after the loaf is baked.

About the Dough: This is a delightful dough to work with. The olives act like natural steam injectors when baked, which makes the crumb soft, tender, and squishy. To support the weight of the olives, I like to stretch and fold the dough during the bulk rise for added height. This step is optional but fun.

DOUGH

50 g (¼ cup) bubbly, active starter

360 g (1½ cups) warm water

470 g (about 4 cups) bread flour

30 g (¼ cup) all-purpose flour

9 g (1½ tsp) fine sea salt

FILLINGS

120 g (1 heaped cup) pitted mixed olives, roughly chopped

2 g (1 tbsp) picked thyme leaves

Zest of 1 lemon

40 g (¼ cup) ground Parmesan cheese

Olive oil, for brushing

80 g (½ cup) grated Parmesan cheese, for topping

A few days before baking, feed your starter until bubbly and active. Store at room temperature until ready to use.

TIP: To complement the earthy notes of this loaf, replace 30 grams (¼ cup) of bread flour with 30 grams (¼ cup) of whole wheat flour. The extra acidity in the whole-grain flour will give the dough a more sour flavor.

MAKE THE DOUGH: In a large bowl, whisk the starter and water together with a fork. Add the flours and salt. Combine to form a stiff dough, then finish mixing by hand to fully incorporate the flour. Cover with a damp towel and let rest for 30 minutes. Replenish your starter with fresh flour and water, and store according to preference.

ADD THE FILLINGS: After the dough has rested, add the olives, thyme, lemon zest, and Parmesan to the bowl. Gently knead the fillings into the dough, about 1 minute. The dough will take on a slight purple-stained hue from the olives.

BULK RISE: Cover the bowl with a damp towel and let rise at room temperature until double in size. This will take about 8 to 10 hours at 70°F (21°C). When ready, the dough will have a few bubbles on the surface and will jiggle a bit when you move the bowl from side to side. *Optional Step:* About 30 minutes into the bulk rise, stretch and fold the dough for added structure and height. Repeat this technique, about 2 to 3 sets, spaced 30 minutes apart (see page 194 for more details).

SHAPE: Remove the dough onto a lightly floured surface. Shape it into an oval and let rest for 5 to 10 minutes. Meanwhile, line a 10-inch (25-cm) oval proofing basket with a towel and dust with flour. With floured hands, gently cup the dough and pull it toward you to tighten its shape. Then place the dough into your basket, seam side up.

SECOND RISE: Cover the dough and let rest until noticeably puffy but not fully risen, about 30 minutes to 1 hour, depending on temperature.

Preheat your oven to 450°F (230°C). Cut a sheet of parchment paper to fit the size of your baking pot.

SCORE: Place the parchment over the dough and invert the basket to release. Sprinkle the dough very lightly with flour and rub the surface to coat. You will be dusting the loaf with cheese later on, so it's best not to go too heavy with the flour at this stage. Make one long, off-center cut down the length of the loaf using a small knife or razor blade. Use the parchment to transfer the dough into the baking pot.

BAKE: Bake the dough on the center rack for 20 minutes, covered. Remove the lid, and continue to bake for 30 minutes. Lift the loaf out of the pot, and finish baking directly on the oven rack for the last 10 minutes. Cool for 1 hour before adding the cheese and cutting into slices.

ADD THE CHEESE: Lightly brush the surface of the loaf with oil. Sprinkle with the Parmesan cheese, patting down gently to stick.

This loaf will stay fresh up to 1 day stored at room temperature in a plastic bag.

SEEDED PUMPKIN CRANBERRY

Makes 1 Loaf

A simple yet artful way to expand your sourdough is to add different purees to the dough. In this case, a generous dollop of silky pumpkin puree stains the crumb a beautiful, brassy orange color. The pumpkin flavor is not very pronounced, but cranberries soaked in fresh orange juice, cinnamon, and spices give the bread that familiar seasonal taste. Enjoy this sourdough on a brisk autumn day or with Thanksgiving leftovers for the full effect. My dad likes to fry day-old slices in a hot skillet with melted butter.

About the Dough: This dough wins the award for most improved. After mixing, it will feel sticky and stiff, more so than usual. Once it rests—the longer the better—the texture will morph into a soft, mousse-like mass. You can't help but want to touch it!

DOUGH

50 g (¼ cup) bubbly, active starter

250 g (1 cup plus 2 tsp) warm water

184 g (¾ cup) good-quality pumpkin puree (not pie filling)

500 g (4 cups plus 2 tbsp) bread flour

9 g (1½ tsp) fine sea salt

FILLINGS

130 g (1 cup) dried cranberries

12 g (1 tbsp) sugar

5 g (1 tsp) pure vanilla extract

Pinch each of ground cinnamon, ginger, and nutmeg

4 clementines or 1 orange

180 g (1½ cups) pumpkin seeds, for coating

A few days before baking, feed your starter until bubbly and active. Store at room temperature until ready to use.

TIP: I've tried many different ways to get nuts and seeds to stick to bread dough. Egg wash, egg white, milk, cream—you name it. The technique outlined is guaranteed for better sticking, and is worth the few extra pumpkin seeds that will inevitably land on the floor.

MAKE THE DOUGH: In a large bowl, whisk the starter, water, and pumpkin puree together with a fork. Add the flour and salt. Mix to combine until a stiff dough forms, then finish by hand until the flour is fully absorbed. Cover the dough with a damp towel and let rest for 45 minutes to 1 hour. Replenish your starter with fresh flour and water, and store according to preference.

Meanwhile, add the cranberries, sugar, vanilla, and spices to a small bowl. Halve the clementines and squeeze the juice over the cranberries. It's okay if the cranberries are not completely submerged. Stir well to combine. Taste one too—they're really good. Do not drain.

ADD THE FILLINGS: After the dough has rested, add the cranberries with their soaking juice to the bowl. Gently knead the fillings to incorporate, about 1 minute.

BULK RISE: Cover the bowl with a damp towel and let rise at room temperature, 70°F (21°C), for about 6 to 8 hours, or until double in size.

SHAPE THE DOUGH AND COAT WITH SEEDS: Remove the dough onto a lightly floured surface. Shape it into an oval and let rest for 5 to 10 minutes. Meanwhile, line a 10-inch (25-cm) oval proofing basket with a towel and set aside. Spread the pumpkin seeds on a damp kitchen towel.

With floured hands, gently cup the dough and pull it toward you to tighten its shape. Then brush the surface and sides of the dough with water. Using a bench scraper, place the dough onto the pumpkin seeds, wet side down. Lift up the sides of the towel and rock it back and forth to coat the dough. Place the dough into your basket, seam side up.

SECOND RISE: Cover the dough, and let rest until puffy but not fully risen, about 30 minutes to 1 hour.

Preheat your oven to 450°F (230°C). Cut a sheet of parchment paper to fit the size of your baking pot.

SCORE: Place the parchment over the dough and invert the basket to release. Make a long cut down the length of the dough using the tip of a small serrated knife or a razor blade. Try to be quick and precise with this one—your blade will inevitably catch on some of the seeds. Use the parchment to transfer the dough into the baking pot.

BAKE: Bake the dough on the center rack for 20 minutes, covered. Remove the lid, and continue to bake for 40 minutes. Additional baking time inside the pot, as opposed to baking directly on the oven rack, will protect the seeds from burning. Cool for 1 hour before slicing.

This loaf will stay fresh up to 1 day stored at room temperature in a plastic bag.

CINNAMON RAISIN SWIRL

Makes 1 Loaf

When I was a kid, my favorite school lunch was cinnamon raisin bread with cream cheese, no crust. This sourdough version is a delightful upgrade and will please both grown-ups and kids alike. Plump raisins and walnuts are added for texture and crunch, and the loaf will make your whole house smell warm and cozy while it bakes.

About the Dough: To create a good swirl, you'll need to stretch the dough into a long, thin rectangle. The longer the rectangle, the more swirls will form in the loaf. It doesn't have to look perfect, but the idea is to keep the cinnamon tucked inside so it doesn't seep out when baked.

DOUGH
50 g (¼ cup) bubbly, active starter
365 g (1½ cups plus 1 tsp) warm water
480 g (4 cups) bread flour
20 g (scant ¼ cup) whole wheat flour
9 g (1½ tsp) fine sea salt

FILLINGS
65 g (⅓ cup) raisins
65 g (½ cup) walnuts

50 g (¼ cup) sugar
6 g (2 tsp) cinnamon

A few days before baking, feed your starter until bubbly and active. Store at room temperature until ready to use.

MAKE THE DOUGH: In a large bowl, whisk the starter and water together with a fork. Add the flours and salt. Cover with a damp towel and let rest for 30 minutes to 1 hour, depending on your schedule. Replenish your starter with fresh flour and water, and store according to preference.

Meanwhile, while the dough is resting, soak the raisins and walnuts in just enough warm water to cover. Drain well before using.

ADD THE FILLINGS: Add the raisins and nuts to the bowl. Gently knead the fillings into the dough to incorporate, about 1 minute. The dough will start to feel slightly sticky at this point; add a sprinkle of flour to adjust the consistency.

BULK RISE: Cover the bowl with a damp towel and let rise at room temperature, 70°F (21°C), until double in size, about 8 to 10 hours.

SHAPE AND ASSEMBLE: Remove the dough onto a lightly floured surface. Let it rest for 10 to 15 minutes. A longer rest at this stage will relax the dough, making it easier to stretch into a rectangle. Line a 10-inch (25-cm) oval proofing basket with a towel and dust with flour. Combine the sugar and cinnamon in a small bowl. Set aside.

With floured hands gently stretch the dough into a long rectangle, about 16 × 8 inches (40 × 20 cm). Lightly brush the surface of the dough with water. Then evenly sprinkle the cinnamon sugar mixture over the top, leaving a 2-inch (5-cm) border at the top and bottom edge and a 1-inch (2.5-cm) border around the sides. With the short end facing you, roll the dough into a log, pinching the ends to seal. Place it into the basket, seam side up.

SECOND RISE: Cover the dough, and let rest until puffy but not fully risen, about 30 minutes to 1 hour.

Preheat your oven to 450°F (230°C). Cut a piece of parchment paper to fit the size of your baking pot.

SCORE: Place the parchment over the dough and invert the basket to release. Rub the surface with flour. Using the tip of a small knife or razor blade, make 2 to 3 diagonal cuts, keeping the depth very shallow to preserve the filling. Use the parchment to transfer the dough into the baking pot.

BAKE: Bake the dough on the center rack for 20 minutes, covered. Remove the lid, and continue to bake for 40 minutes. When finished, remove the loaf to a wire rack and cool for 1 hour before slicing.

To maximize freshness, store this loaf in a plastic bag at room temperature for up to 1 day.

CHOCOLATE PEANUT BUTTER CHIP

Makes 1 Loaf

Dark chocolate and peanut butter. Could there be a better combination? What's unique about this sourdough is that dark cocoa powder is added to the dough. It's rich and chocolaty, and it gives the loaf the most beautiful color. While this loaf is not necessarily sweet aside from the peanut butter and chocolate chips, a whimsical dusting of powdered sugar blankets the almond-adorned crust. This smells so good that you'll want to eat the dough.

About the Dough: After mixing, this dough will start out very stiff, due to the cocoa powder. But after a long rest—go for the full hour if you have the time—it will become incredibly soft and supple. The final loaf will feel a bit heavier than most to account for all of the delicious fillings.

DOUGH

50 g (¼ cup) bubbly, active starter

375 g (1½ cups plus 1 tbsp) warm water

480 g (4 cups) bread flour

20 g (¼ cup) cocoa powder

9 g (1½ tsp) fine sea salt

FILLINGS

90 g (½ cup) peanut butter chips

90 g (½ cup) semi-sweet chocolate chips

180 g (1½ cups) flaked almonds

Powdered sugar, for dusting

A few days before baking, feed your starter until bubbly and active. Store at room temperature until ready to use.

TIP: I use Hershey's Special Dark Cocoa for my chocolate sourdoughs. It's a blend of natural and Dutch process cocoa, and it gives the bread a rich, dark color.

MAKE THE DOUGH: In a large bowl, whisk the starter and water together with a fork. Add the flour, cocoa powder, and salt. Mix to combine, then finish by hand to form a rough dough. It will feel very dense and sticky. Cover with a damp towel and let rest for 45 minutes to 1 hour. Replenish your starter with fresh flour and water, and store according to preference.

ADD THE FILLINGS: After the dough has rested, add the peanut butter chips and chocolate chips to the bowl. Gently knead the fillings into the dough to incorporate, about 1 minute.

BULK RISE: Cover the bowl with a damp towel and let rise until double in size, about 8 to 10 hours or more, at 70°F (21°C). The dough will look puffy and nicely domed when ready.

SHAPE THE DOUGH AND COAT WITH ALMONDS: Remove the dough onto a lightly floured surface. Shape it into a round and let rest for 5 to 10 minutes. Meanwhile, line an 8-inch (20-cm) bowl or proofing basket with a towel and set aside. Spread the almonds on a damp kitchen towel.

With floured hands, gently cup the dough and pull it toward you in a circular motion to tighten its shape. Then lightly brush the surface and sides of the dough with water. Using a bench scraper, place the dough onto the almonds, wet side down. Lift up the sides of the towel and rock it back and forth to coat the dough. Place the dough into your bowl, seam side up.

SECOND RISE: Cover the dough, and let rest until puffy but not fully risen, about 30 minutes to 1 hour.

Preheat your oven to 450°F (230°C). Cut a sheet of parchment paper to fit the size of your baking pot.

Right before baking, place the parchment over the dough and invert the bowl to release. Use the parchment to transfer the dough into the baking pot. *Note:* This dough is generally left unscored, although it can be scored, if you prefer.

BAKE: Bake the dough on the center rack for 20 minutes, covered. Remove the lid, and continue to bake for 40 minutes. Transfer the loaf to a wire rack and cool for 1 hour before slicing. Dust liberally with powdered sugar to serve.

This loaf will stay fresh up to 1 day, stored in a plastic bag at room temperature.

PICKLED JALAPEÑO, CHEDDAR, and CHIVE

Makes 1 Loaf

Tangy, spicy pickled jalapeños steal the show in this sourdough. When combined with oniony chives, your bread will smell like a fajita in the oven. It's incredible. Cheddar cheese provides a nice, sharp contrast in flavor, although I've made this with mild and sweet Colby Jack, and it's just as good. This is a great loaf to share with friends or serve toasted with cream cheese for a satisfying mid-afternoon snack.

About the Dough: The bulky weight of the cubed cheese can sometimes bog down the dough while it rises. Make sure to cube the cheese into very small pieces for the best results. Otherwise, be patient until the dough has doubled in size.

DOUGH

50 g (¼ cup) bubbly, active starter

365 g (1½ cups plus 1 tsp) warm water

280 g (2⅓ cups) bread flour

200 g (1⅔ cups) all-purpose flour

20 g (scant ¼ cup) white whole wheat flour or regular whole wheat flour

9 g (1½ tsp) fine sea salt

FILLINGS

50 g (⅓ cup) whole pickled jalapeños

135 g (1 heaped cup) cheddar or Colby Jack cheese, cut into ¼-inch (6.3-mm) cubes

12 g (¼ cup) minced chives

A few days before baking, feed your starter until bubbly and active. Store at room temperature until ready to use.

A NOTE ON FLOUR

A blend of flours is used to create a unique texture and flavor in this sourdough. Whole-grain flour adds extra tang and nuttiness, all-purpose flour adds a fluffy texture, and high-protein bread flour helps to boost the loaf's rise.

MAKE THE DOUGH: In a large bowl, whisk the starter and water together with a fork. Add the flours and salt. Combine to form a rough dough, then finish mixing by hand to fully incorporate the flour. Cover with a damp towel and let rest for 30 minutes. Meanwhile, replenish your starter with fresh flour and water, and store according to preference.

ADD THE FILLINGS: After the dough has rested, add the jalapeños, cheddar, and chives to the bowl. Gently knead the fillings into the dough, about 1 minute.

BULK RISE: Cover the dough with a damp towel and let rise at room temperature until double in size. This will take about 8 to 10 hours at 70°F (21°C).

SHAPE: Coax the dough onto a lightly floured work surface. Shape it into a round or oval and let rest for 5 to 10 minutes. Line an 8-inch (20-cm) bowl or 10-inch (24-cm) oval proofing basket with a towel and dust with flour. Cup the dough and gently tighten according to your desired shape. Place into your proofing vessel, seam side up.

SECOND RISE: Cover the dough and let rest until puffy but not fully risen, about 30 minutes to 1 hour.

Preheat your oven to 450°F (230°C). Cut a sheet of parchment paper to fit the size of your baking pot.

SCORE: Place the parchment over the dough and invert the proofing vessel to release. Sprinkle the dough with flour and rub gently to coat. Using the tip of a small serrated knife or a razor blade, choose one of the scoring patterns on page 195. Use the parchment to transfer the dough into the baking pot.

BAKE: Bake the dough on the center rack for 20 minutes, covered. Remove the lid, and continue to bake for 30 minutes. Lift the loaf out of the pot, and finish baking directly on the oven rack for the last 10 minutes. Transfer to a wire rack and cool for 1 hour before slicing.

This loaf will stay fresh up to 1 to 2 days, stored at room temperature in a plastic bag.

ROASTED GARLIC *and* ROSEMARY

Makes 1 Loaf

This is one of my go-to loaves for entertaining. Soft, sweet, and caramelized to perfection, roasted garlic adds beautiful depth of flavor, intensified with hints of fresh rosemary. This bread needs nothing more than a pool of rich, silky olive oil for dunking. Any leftovers make brilliant toasted cheese sandwiches with a crunchy green salad on the side.

About the Dough: To make the most of your time, you can roast the garlic while the dough is resting, or you can make it in advance and freeze until ready to use. The natural sugars might boost the dough's rise time, so keep an eye on it if you're around.

ROASTED GARLIC
1 large head of fresh garlic
Olive oil, for coating

DOUGH
50 g (¼ cup) bubbly, active starter
365 g (1½ cups plus 1 tsp) warm water
480 g (4 cups) bread flour
20 g (scant ¼ cup) whole wheat flour
9 g (1½ tsp) fine sea salt
1 g (2 tsp) chopped rosemary

A few days before baking, feed your starter until bubbly and active. Store at room temperature until ready to use.

ROAST THE GARLIC: Preheat your oven to 400°F (200°C). Lay the garlic on its side, and slice off the top third to reveal the inside cloves. Drizzle with olive oil to coat and wrap the garlic in foil. Roast on a sheet pan for 45 minutes to 1 hour. The garlic will be soft and caramelized when ready. Cool slightly before adding to the dough.

MAKE THE DOUGH: In a large bowl, whisk the starter and water together with a fork. Add the flours and salt. Combine to form a rough dough, then mix by hand to mop up all of the dry bits of flour. Cover with a damp towel and let rest for 30 minutes. Meanwhile, replenish your starter with fresh flour and water, and store according to preference.

ADD THE GARLIC: After the dough has rested, squeeze the roasted garlic cloves directly into the bowl. Add the chopped rosemary. Gently knead the dough to incorporate, tucking in the cloves as you go, about 30 seconds.

BULK RISE: Cover the dough with a damp towel and let rise at room temperature until double in size, about 8 to 10 hours at 70°F (21°C).

SHAPE: Remove the dough onto a lightly floured work surface. Shape it into a round and let rest for 5 to 10 minutes. Meanwhile, line an 8-inch (20-cm) bowl or proofing basket with a towel and dust with flour. With floured hands, gently cup the dough and pull it toward you in a circular motion to tighten its shape. Place the dough into the bowl, seam side up.

SECOND RISE: Cover the dough and let rest until puffy but not fully risen, about 30 minutes to 1 hour.

Preheat your oven to 450°F (230°C). Cut a sheet of parchment paper to fit the size of your baking pot.

SCORE: Place the parchment over the dough and invert the bowl to release. Dust the dough with flour and rub it in gently with your hands. Using the tip of a small paring knife or razor blade, make eight 4-inch (10-cm) long cuts around the dough. Or choose a scoring pattern from page 195. Use the parchment to transfer the dough into the baking pot.

BAKE: Bake the dough on the center rack for 20 minutes, covered. Remove the lid, and continue to bake for 30 minutes. Lift the loaf out of the pot, and finish baking directly on the oven rack for the last 10 minutes. Transfer to a wire rack, and cool for 1 hour before slicing.

This loaf will stay fresh for 1 to 2 days, stored at room temperature in a plastic bag.

STICKY DATE, WALNUT, and ORANGE

Makes 1 Loaf

Soft, sweet, sticky dates melt into the crumb, which is the most fantastic sensation in this sourdough. You'll notice it after just one bite. Paired with fresh clementine zest and toasted walnuts, the combination creates beautiful, aromatic flavor. This loaf goes really well with an assorted cured meat and cheese platter.

About the Dough: This is a dense and hearty dough, due to the addition of whole wheat flour, dates, and walnuts. For best results, make sure to chop the walnuts and dates into small pieces, so the weight doesn't drag down the dough as it rises. This dough was proofed in a well-floured proofing basket, which adds a whimsical decoration along the outside crust.

DOUGH

50 g (¼ cup) bubbly, active starter

350 g (1⅓ cups plus 2 tbsp) warm water

100 g (¾ cup plus 1 tbsp) whole wheat flour

100 g (¾ cup plus 1 tbsp) bread flour

200 g (1⅔ cups) all-purpose flour

9 g (1½ tsp) fine sea salt

FILLINGS

65 g (½ cup) chopped walnuts

6 medjool dates, pitted and diced into small pieces

Zest of 4 clementines or 1 large orange

A few days before baking, feed your starter until bubbly and active. Store at room temperature until ready to use.

TIP: If your dates are dry and crackly, soak them (whole) in hot water before adding to the dough. If you happen to have plump and fresh dates, there's no need to soak them first. However, they might be difficult to cut without sticking to your knife. Lightly oil your knife to make dicing easier, or simply tear the dates into small pieces with your hands.

MAKE THE DOUGH: In a large bowl, whisk the starter and water together with a fork. Add the flours and salt. Combine to form a rough dough, mopping up any dry bits of flour as you go. Cover with a damp towel and let rest for 45 minutes to 1 hour. Replenish your starter with fresh flour and water, and store according to preference.

Meanwhile, warm a nonstick pan over low heat. Toast the walnuts until fragrant, stirring occasionally, about 3 to 4 minutes. Once cool enough to handle, chop into small pieces.

ADD THE FILLINGS: After the dough has rested, add the toasted walnuts and dates to the bowl. Zest the clementines into the dough. Gently knead the dough to incorporate, about 1 minute.

BULK RISE: Cover the dough with a damp towel and let rise at room temperature, 70°F (21°C), until double in size, about 8 to 10 hours or more.

SHAPE: Remove the dough onto a lightly floured work surface. Shape the dough into an oval and let rest for 5 to 10 minutes. Meanwhile, generously dust a 10-inch (25-cm) oval proofing basket with flour. With floured hands, gently cup the dough and pull it toward you to tighten its shape. Place the dough into your basket, seam side up.

SECOND RISE: Cover the dough and let rest until puffy but not fully risen, about 30 minutes to 1 hour.

Preheat your oven to 450°F (230°C). Cut a sheet of parchment paper to fit the size of your baking pot.

SCORE: Place the parchment over the dough and invert the basket to release. Make a long cut down the length of the dough, using the tip of a small knife or razor blade. Use the parchment to transfer the dough into the baking pot.

BAKE: Bake the dough on the center rack for 20 minutes, covered. Remove the lid, and continue to bake for 30 minutes. Lift the bread out of the pot, and finish baking directly on the oven rack for the last 10 minutes. Transfer to a wire rack and cool for 1 hour before slicing.

This loaf will stay fresh up to 1 to 2 days, stored at room temperature in a plastic bag.

PAN LOAVES *and* SANDWICH BREAD

In addition to crusty artisan loaves, sourdough makes the best sandwich bread and pan loaves, including Soft Honey Whole Wheat (page 65), buttery Light and Fluffy Brioche (page 70), and wholesome Overnight Danish Rye Bread (page 73). Most of the same sourdough baking steps apply. All you need is a loaf pan (or two) to get started—it's that simple. Just a heads-up: Once you start making these loaves at home, you will never depend on store-bought again. Good sandwich bread is a staple in every house, and there's nothing more rewarding than baking it yourself. Feel free to double any of these recipes to freeze.

COUNTRY FARMHOUSE WHITE

Makes 1 Loaf

This loaf is everything you love about sourdough. It's incredibly soft and chewy, and its flavorful crumb is just waiting to be topped with your favorite sandwich fillings. The addition of oil conditions the dough and, in my opinion, keeps the bread fresh for longer. This bread is not enriched with milk or eggs, so for those with dietary restrictions, it's a home run without sacrifice.

About the Dough: Sandwich doughs are typically drier, which helps to create a tight, uniform crumb. If you find that the dough is too stiff to mix by hand, use a stand mixer instead.

65 g (⅓ cup) bubbly, active starter

300 g (1¼ cups) warm water

12 g (1 tbsp) sugar

15 g (1 tbsp) oil, plus more for coating the pan

400 g (3⅓ cups) bread flour

100 g (¾ cup plus 1 tbsp) all-purpose flour

9 g (1½ tsp) fine seat salt

A few days before baking, feed your starter until bubbly and active. Store at room temperature until ready to use.

MAKE THE DOUGH: In a large bowl, whisk the starter, water, sugar, and oil together with a fork. Add the flours and salt. Combine to form a rough dough, then finish mixing by hand to absorb all of the dry bits of flour. Cover the dough with a damp towel and let rest for 30 minutes to 1 hour, depending on your schedule. Meanwhile, replenish your starter with fresh flour and water, and store according to preference.

After the dough has rested, work it into a semi-smooth ball, about 20 seconds. The dough will feel stiff but much softer than earlier.

BULK RISE: Cover the bowl with a damp towel and let rise at room temperature, 70°F (21°C), until double in size, about 8 to 10 hours.

SHAPE: Remove the dough onto a lightly floured work surface. Gently dimple the surface of the dough with your fingertips to release any large air bubbles. Roll the dough into a log, tucking the ends underneath. Let rest for 5 to 10 minutes. Meanwhile, lightly coat a 9 × 5-inch (23 × 13-cm) loaf pan with oil. With floured hands, cup the dough and pull it toward you to tighten its shape. Place into your loaf pan, seam side down.

SECOND RISE: Cover the dough, and let rest until it has risen about 1 inch (2.5 cm) above the rim of pan. This will take about 1 to 2 hours, depending on temperature.

Preheat your oven to 375°F (190°C).

BAKE: Bake the dough on the center rack for about 40 to 45 minutes. The loaf will be beautifully risen and golden brown when ready. Cool in the pan for 10 minutes, then transfer the loaf to a wire rack to cool completely.

This sandwich loaf will stay fresh up to 3 to 5 days, stored in a plastic bag at room temperature.

VARIATION: For a richer sourdough, replace the water with warm milk, whole or 2%, and swap the oil for melted unsalted butter.

SOFT HONEY WHOLE WHEAT

Makes 1 Loaf

Settling on a whole wheat loaf that was both soft and delicious wasn't easy. Any time you add whole wheat flour to bread, you run the risk of the loaf becoming dry and dense. Want to know my secret? Plenty of sourdough starter for strength, milk to soften the crumb, and just a touch of honey for sweetness. The best part is the melted butter brushed over the top when finished. Work this loaf into your baking routine, and bake several to freeze for the week.

About the Dough: For lighter bread, let the dough rest for a full hour before the bulk rise. This will jumpstart gluten development without kneading, adding great texture and height to the finished loaf. I also recommend using a stand mixer if you have one, for added air.

150 g (¾ cup) bubbly, active starter

270 g (1 cup plus 2 tbsp) warm milk, whole or 2%

30 g (2 tbsp) warm water

40 g (2 tbsp) honey

30 g (2 tbsp) oil, plus more for coating the pan

120 g (1 cup) whole wheat flour or white whole wheat flour

360 g (3 cups) bread flour

9 g (1½ tsp) fine sea salt

14 g (1 tbsp) unsalted butter, melted

A few days before baking, feed your starter until bubbly and active. Store at room temperature until ready to use.

MAKE THE DOUGH: In a large bowl, whisk the starter, milk, water, honey, and oil together with a fork. Add the flours and salt. Mix to combine, then finish by hand until a rough dough forms. Cover with a damp towel and let rest for 45 minutes to 1 hour, depending on your schedule. Replenish your starter with fresh flour and water, and store according to preference.

After the dough has rested, gently work it into a semi-smooth ball, about 15 to 20 seconds. The dough will feel supple and smooth when it comes together.

BULK RISE: Cover the bowl with a damp towel and let rise at room temperature, 70°F (21°C), until double in size, about 6 to 8 hours. The dough will look nice and domed when ready.

SHAPE: Remove the dough onto a lightly floured work surface. Gently dimple the surface with your fingertips to release any large air bubbles. Roll the dough into a log, tucking the ends underneath. Let rest for 5 to 10 minutes. Meanwhile, lightly coat a 9 × 5-inch (23 × 13-cm) loaf pan with oil. With floured hands, cup the dough and pull it toward you to tighten its shape. Place into your loaf pan, seam side down.

SECOND RISE: Cover the dough and let rest until it has risen about 1 inch (2.5 cm) above the rim of pan, about 1½ to 2 hours, depending on temperature.

Preheat your oven to 375°F (190°C).

BAKE: Bake the dough on the center rack for 40 to 45 minutes. When finished, remove the loaf from the oven and brush the crust with the melted butter. Cool in the pan for 10 minutes, then transfer the loaf to a wire rack to cool completely before slicing.

This loaf is best consumed within 1 to 2 days, stored in a plastic bag at room temperature.

A NOTE ON FLOUR

One of my favorite flours to work with is white whole wheat. It is milled from a wheat variety that's lighter in color and more mild in taste than traditional whole wheat flour—it's *not* bleached wheat flour. You can replace whole wheat for white whole wheat for any recipe in this book.

SATURDAY MORNING FRUIT *and* NUT TOAST

Makes 1 Loaf

There's a baker's shelf in my kitchen with several mismatched jars of dried fruits and nuts. It's both decorative and functional, but mostly inspiring for sourdough. I came up with this recipe using bits and pieces of what I had, but I quickly learned that chewy, sweet apricots and nutty sunflower seeds are a powerhouse combination! This is a wonderful, hearty loaf. Imagine a thick, toasted, buttered slice with a frothy cappuccino at the ready.

About the Dough: For best results, make sure to weigh your ingredients and chop the dried fruit into small pieces, as they will plump up when soaked. I like to make this dough on Friday evening, to rise at room temperature overnight. On Saturday morning, I quickly shape and bake the dough, just in time for breakfast.

DOUGH

65 g (⅓ cup) bubbly, active starter
325 g (1⅓ cups plus 1 tsp) warm water
500 g (4 cups plus 2 tbsp) bread flour
9 g (1½ tsp) fine sea salt

FILLINGS

100 g (about 1 cup) mixed dried fruit such as cherries, blueberries, golden raisins, and cranberries, roughly chopped
50 g (about 5 whole) dried apricots, diced
50 g (⅓ cup) sunflower seeds
10 g (2 tsp) pure vanilla extract
24 g (2 tbsp) sugar
1 g (½ tsp) cinnamon

Butter, for coating the pan

A few days before baking, feed your starter until bubbly and active. Store at room temperature until ready to use.

MAKE THE DOUGH: In a large bowl, whisk the starter and water together with a fork. Add the flour and salt. Mix to combine, then finish by hand to form a rough and shaggy dough. Cover with a damp towel and let rest for 45 minutes to 1 hour, depending on your schedule. A long rest at this stage will make the fillings easier to incorporate. Replenish your starter with fresh flour and water, and store according to preference.

Meanwhile, soak the dried fruit, apricots, and sunflower seeds in just enough warm water to cover. Add the vanilla, sugar, and cinnamon, and stir to combine. Drain well before using.

ADD THE FILLINGS: After the dough has rested, add the fruit mixture to the bowl. Gently knead the dough to incorporate, about 1 to 2 minutes.

BULK RISE: Cover the bowl with a damp towel and let rise at room temperature until double in size, about 8 to 10 hours or more at 70°F (21°C).

SHAPE: Remove the dough onto a lightly floured work surface. Gently dimple the surface with your fingertips to release some of the air. Roll the dough into a log, tucking the ends underneath. Let rest for 5 to 10 minutes. Meanwhile, lightly coat a 9 × 5-inch (23 × 13-cm) loaf pan with butter. With floured hands, cup the dough and pull it toward you to tighten its shape. Transfer to your loaf pan, seam side down.

SECOND RISE: Cover the dough, and let it rise until it reaches about 1 inch (2.5 cm) above the rim of pan. This will take about 1 to 2 hours, depending on temperature.

Preheat your oven to 450°F (230°C).

BAKE: Place the dough on the center rack and reduce the heat to 400°F (200°C). Bake for 45 to 50 minutes. Check on the loaf halfway through baking, and tent loosely with foil if the fruit is browning too quickly. Cool the loaf in the pan for 10 minutes. Transfer to a wire rack to finish cooling before cutting into slices.

The moisture in the dried fruit will keep this loaf fresh for 3 to 4 days. Store at room temperature in a plastic bag.

MULTIGRAIN SANDWICH BREAD

Makes 1 Loaf

Don't you just feel healthier saying the word "multigrain"? You are going to love the texture and taste of this feel-good sourdough. What makes it unique is the addition of coconut oil, which brings out all the natural nutty flavors and gives the bread a warm, wonderful aroma. This multigrain makes the best toast, too, with almond butter, sliced banana, and a drizzle of orange-blossom honey.

About the Dough: Multigrains must be soaked prior to using; otherwise, they will rob all of the moisture in your dough. Because of this, this sourdough might need a few extra minutes of baking time. However, in return, your loaf will stay fresh for longer. Also worth noting: Use a touch of oil to coat your work surface when shaping the dough. This technique can be used in lieu of flour for sticky doughs, like this one.

DOUGH

50 g (¼ cup) bubbly, active starter

300 g (1¼ cups) warm water

20 g (1 tbsp) honey

45 g (3 tbsp) melted coconut oil, plus more for coating

50 g (about ⅓ cup plus 1 tbsp) whole wheat flour

450 g (3¾ cups) bread flour

9 g (1½ tsp) fine sea salt

MULTIGRAINS

70 g (½ cup) Harvest Grains Blend or 10-grain hot cereal

240 g (1 cup) hot water

Small handful of rolled oats, for topping the loaf

A few days before baking, feed your starter until bubbly and active. Store at room temperature until ready to use.

TIP: Harvest Grains Blend or 10-grain multigrain hot cereal is available in most grocery stores or online. See the Source List (page 196) for details.

MAKE THE DOUGH: In a large bowl, whisk the starter, water, honey and oil together with a fork. Add the flours and salt. Combine to form a rough dough, then mix by hand to fully incorporate the flour. Cover with a damp towel and let rest for 30 minutes. Replenish your starter with fresh flour and water, and store according to preference.

Meanwhile, add the multigrains to a bowl and cover with 240 grams (1 cup) of hot water. Allow to soak while the dough is resting. Drain well before using.

ADD THE MULTIGRAINS: Add the grains to the bowl. Gently knead the dough to incorporate, about 1 minute. The dough will feel wet and slippery at first, but it will become easier to work with as you continue to move it around.

BULK RISE: Cover the bowl with a damp towel and let rise at room temperature until double in size. This will take about 6 to 8 hours at 70°F (21°C).

SHAPE: Remove the dough onto a lightly oiled surface. Press your fingertips into the dough just a few times to release any large air bubbles. Roll the dough into a log, tucking the ends underneath. Let rest for 5 to 10 minutes. Meanwhile, lightly coat a 9 × 5-inch (23 × 13-cm) loaf pan with coconut oil. Gently cup the dough and pull it toward you to tighten its shape. Place into your loaf pan, seam side down.

SECOND RISE: Cover the dough, and let rest until it has risen to about 1 inch (2.5 cm) above the rim of the pan, about 1 to 2 hours, depending on temperature.

Preheat your oven to 450°F (230°C). Lightly brush the dough with water and sprinkle with the oats to coat.

BAKE: Place the dough on the center rack, and reduce the heat to 400°F (200°C). Bake for about 50 to 60 minutes. Cool in the pan for 10 minutes, then transfer the loaf to a wire rack to cool completely before slicing.

The moisture from the soaked grains will keep this loaf fresh for 2 to 3 days. Store at room temperature in a plastic bag to maximize freshness.

LIGHT *and* FLUFFY BRIOCHE

Makes 1 Loaf

Brioche, a classic French bread enriched with butter and eggs, ranks high in a category all its own. Its rich, tender, velvety crumb is a cross between bread and cake. I sent my son to school with a slice of brioche for lunch and he said, "Mommy, your bread is outstanding!" He's five years old.

About the Dough: Brioche is notoriously sticky. It's best to use a stand mixer to incorporate some much-needed air and offset the richness of the dough. You'll also need a warm spot for it to rise, such as a cozy cabinet or near a heater. Chill this dough overnight once it has risen; sticky dough is much easier to shape when chilled and firm.

DOUGH

500 g (4 cups plus 2 tbsp) bread flour

9 g (1½ tsp) fine sea salt

50 g (¼ cup) sugar

250 g (1¼ cups) bubbly, active starter

3 large eggs, lightly beaten

120 g (½ cup) warm milk, whole or 2%

113 g (8 tbsp) cold, unsalted butter, cut into small cubes, plus more for coating

EGG WASH

1 large egg

Splash of water

A few days before baking, feed your starter until bubbly and active. Store at room temperature until ready to use.

ROLL VARIATION: Shape the dough into 10 balls, about 106 grams (3¾ oz) each. Bake on a lined sheet pan for 20 to 25 minutes at 400°F (200°C) until golden brown.

MAKE THE DOUGH: Add the flour, salt, and sugar to the bowl of a stand mixer fitted with the paddle attachment. Mix briefly to combine. With the machine running, gradually add the starter, eggs, and warm milk. Mix on low speed until a sticky, shaggy dough forms and all of the flour is fully absorbed, about 2 to 3 minutes. Scrape down the sides of the bowl as needed. Cover and rest the dough for 15 to 30 minutes. Meanwhile, replenish your starter with fresh flour and water, and store according to preference.

ADD THE BUTTER: Fit the stand mixer with the dough hook attachment. On low speed, add the butter one cube at a time, waiting 10 to 20 seconds before the next addition. Increase to medium speed, and knead the dough until the butter is fully incorporated, about 5 to 7 minutes or more. When ready, the dough will look shiny and smooth but will not come together into a ball. It will also feel warm to the touch. Scrape down the sides of the bowl when finished.

BULK RISE: With floured hands, transfer the dough to a new, lightly buttered bowl. Cover with a damp towel and find a warm spot for the dough to rise. This will take about 5 to 8 hours or more, depending on temperature. Once fully risen, cover the dough with lightly oiled plastic wrap and transfer to the fridge. Chill overnight.

SHAPE: In the morning, lightly coat a 9 × 5-inch (23 × 13-cm) loaf pan with butter. Remove the cold dough onto a well-floured work surface. It will feel very firm from the chilled butter. To shape, you have two options: For a traditional-style loaf, pat the dough into a rectangle and roll into a log. Place into your loaf pan, seam side down. Or divide the dough into four pieces, about 265 g (about 9 oz) each. Working with one piece at a time, gather the ends, flip the dough over, and gently roll into a ball. Stagger the dough, seam side down, into your loaf pan. The dough will fit snugly.

SECOND RISE: Cover the dough with a damp towel and let rise until puffy, about 1½ to 2 hours or more. Because the dough is cold, it might take longer than usual to puff up and become less dense. If so, you can always return the dough to the warm spot you used for the bulk rise. The dough is ready when it has risen about 1 inch (2.5 cm) above the rim of the loaf pan.

Preheat your oven to 400°F (200°C). Combine the egg with a splash of water and brush the dough until well coated in the egg wash.

BAKE: Bake the dough on the center rack for about 40 to 45 minutes. If the loaf starts to brown too quickly, loosely tent with foil. The loaf will be rich, golden brown, and shiny when finished. Cool in the pan for 10 minutes, then remove to a wire rack to cool completely before cutting into slices.

Brioche will stay fresh up to 2 days, stored at room temperature, covered in plastic wrap.

OVERNIGHT DANISH RYE BREAD

Makes 1 Loaf

My first experience with this hearty, dense-in-a-good-way bread was at a party, served open face, piled high with smoked salmon, creamy butter, shaved cucumbers, and dill—delicious! I was inspired to create my own version, so this sourdough is made with mostly with rye flour and filled with plenty of crunchy nuts and seeds. I guarantee you'll be hooked after just one bite. Try a slice with the suggested serving options or with creamy hummus and juicy tomatoes for a delicious, healthy snack. .

About the Dough: Rye flour doesn't contain very much gluten, so this dough will not become soft and springy after mixing or resting. It's more like thick, gingerbread cake batter. This dough needs to rest for 24 hours, which will give the finished loaf a wonderful tangy flavor. It can be made in the morning and baked the following day.

DOUGH
150 g (¾ cup) bubbly, active starter
360 g (1½ cups) warm water
20 g (1 tbsp) unsulphured molasses
210 g (2⅓ cups) white rye flour
150 g (1¼ cups) bread flour
30 g (¼ cup) pumpernickel flour
5 g (1 tsp) fine sea salt

FILLINGS
60 g (½ cup) sunflower seeds
60 g (½ cup) pumpkin seeds
30 g (¼ cup) flaked almonds
45 g (¼ cup) golden flax seeds
20 g (2 tbsp) sesame seeds

Oil, for coating the pan
Extra seeds, for sprinkling

SERVING OPTIONS
Smoked salmon
Cucumbers, thinly sliced
Red onions, thinly sliced
Unsalted butter
Fresh dill

A few days before baking, feed your starter until bubbly and active. Store at room temperature until ready to use.

MAKE THE DOUGH: In a large bowl, whisk the starter, water, and molasses together. Add the flours and salt. Stir with a wooden spoon to combine. The texture will be noticeably wet and sticky and will feel like mud. Add the fillings to the bowl and continue to stir until thoroughly incorporated. Replenish your starter with fresh flour and water, and store according to preference.

BULK RISE: Cover the dough with plastic wrap, and let rise at room temperature for 24 hours, about 70°F (21°C). The dough will increase in size, although it may not double, and will look spongy and bubbly on the surface.

ASSEMBLE: Lightly coat a 9 × 5-inch (23 × 13-cm) loaf pan with oil. Scoop the dough into the loaf pan, using a rubber spatula to scrape down the sides of the bowl. Smooth out the surface as best you can. Sprinkle with extra seeds for decoration.

SECOND RISE: Cover the dough and let rest until it has risen almost to the top of the pan, about 1½ to 2 hours. The dough will still look thick and dense at this stage.

Preheat your oven to 400°F (200°C).

BAKE: Bake the loaf on the center rack for about 1 hour and 20 minutes. This loaf won't rise very much, so don't panic when you peek through the oven door. The top will become golden brown and the sides will pull away from the edges of the pan when ready. Remove from the oven and cool for 10 minutes. For best texture, transfer the loaf to a wire rack for several hours to cool completely.

This Danish rye bread will stay fresh up to 1 week, stored at room temperature and covered tightly in plastic wrap.

WHOLE GRAINS *and* SPECIALTY FLOURS

Whole grains and specialty flours are prized for their toasty, earthy flavors. Their natural complexity is a perfect match for sourdough. Not to mention, they boast a wide range of health benefits. They're packed with protein, fiber, and plenty of nutrients. Some are even low in gluten.

With sourdough, however, these flours require a slightly different approach due to their unique nature. They tend to drink in more water, rise faster, and do not bake up quite as high when compared to all-white loaves. For more oven spring, I recommend stretching and folding the dough throughout the bulk rise for added support. In this chapter, you'll learn the subtle—and not so subtle—distinctions between a variety of flours, including whole wheat, spelt, golden semolina, pumpernickel, and rye. It's fun to explore and experiment, and you'll have no trouble finding everything you need in the grocery store or online.

WHOLE WHEAT SOURDOUGH

Makes 1 Loaf

Ah, whole wheat bread. One false move and you could end up with a loaf that tastes like firewood. The secret to lighter, edible loaves is to understand whole-grain flours themselves. Typically, the bran or germ is included in the flour, which tends to weigh down the dough. You won't get mile-high oven spring, but you will get rich, deep, nutty flavor, making whole-grain bread what we crave.

This recipe combines whole wheat flour with all-purpose and bread flour for volume. In my experience, it's best to start with a smaller percentage of whole-grain flour and work your way up. Otherwise, your sourdough might be too dense for your liking.

About the Dough: Whole wheat flour tends to absorb more water than white flour; give the dough extra time to rest before the bulk rise for best texture.

50 g (¼ cup) bubbly, active starter

375 g (1½ cups plus 1 tbsp) warm water

20 g (1 tbsp) honey

120 g (1 cup) whole wheat flour

190 g (1½ cups plus 1 tbsp) all-purpose flour

190 g (1½ cups plus 1 tbsp) bread flour

9 g (1½ tsp) fine sea salt

A few days before baking, feed your starter until bubbly and active. Store at room temperature until ready to use.

MAKE THE DOUGH: In a large bowl, whisk the starter, water, and honey together with a fork. Add the flours and salt. Mix with your hands until a rough, sticky dough forms. Cover with a damp towel and let rest for 45 minutes to 1 hour, depending on your schedule. Replenish your starter with fresh flour and water, and store according to preference.

After the dough has rested, work the mass into a semi-smooth ball, about 15 to 20 seconds.

BULK RISE: Cover the dough with a damp towel and let rise at room temperature, 70°F (21°C), about 6 to 8 hours. The dough will just about double in size when ready, and jiggle a bit when you move the bowl from side to side. *Optional Step:* About 30 minutes into the bulk rise, stretch and fold the dough for added structure and height. Repeat this technique, about 2 to 3 sets, spaced 30 minutes apart (page 194).

SHAPE: Remove the dough onto a lightly floured work surface. Shape it into a round and let rest for 5 to 10 minutes. Line an 8-inch (20-cm) bowl or proofing basket with a towel and dust with flour. With floured hands, gently cup the dough and pull it toward you in a circular motion to tighten its shape. Place the dough into your bowl, seam side up.

SECOND RISE: Cover the dough and let rest until puffy but not fully risen, about 30 minutes to 1 hour.

Preheat your oven to 450°F (230°C). Cut a sheet of parchment paper to fit the size of your baking pot.

SCORE: Place the parchment over the dough and invert the bowl to release. Generously sprinkle the dough with flour and rub the surface with your hands. Using the tip of a razor blade, score the dough with the bird wings pattern on page 195, or any way you'd like. Then use the parchment to transfer the dough into the baking pot.

BAKE: Bake the dough on the center rack for 20 minutes, covered. Remove the lid, and continue to bake for 30 minutes. Lift the loaf out of the pot, and finish baking directly on the rack for the last 10 minutes. Transfer to a wire rack and cool for 1 hour before slicing.

This loaf is best enjoyed on the same day it's baked. Store in a plastic bag at room temperature to maximize freshness, up to 1 day.

GOLDEN FLAX *and* SPELT

Makes 1 Loaf

For this loaf, spelt joins forces with golden flax seeds to create the ultimate superfood sourdough. Spelt, an ancient grain related to wheat, has become increasingly popular in baking. Its mild, nutty, and slightly sweet flavor lends itself well to a variety of applications. It's also not as bitter as some whole-grain flours. Flax seeds, high in omega-3 fatty acids, add a playful, springy texture to the dough. Once the bread is baked, its aroma will tantalize your senses with its deep earthy notes.

About the Dough: Because spelt flour is low in gluten, bread flour and all-purpose are added to create volume and support. Also worth noting: Flax seeds must be soaked prior to using. Otherwise, they will drink up all the water in your dough.

50 g (¼ cup) bubbly, active starter

365 g (1½ cups plus 1 tsp) warm water

180 g (about 1¾ cups) whole spelt flour

150 g (1¼ cups) bread flour

150 g (1¼ cups) all-purpose flour

9 g (1½ tsp) fine sea salt

60 g (about ⅓ cup) golden flax seeds

Oil, for coating

A few days before baking, feed your starter until bubbly and active. Store at room temperature until ready to use.

A NOTE ON FLOUR

When shopping for spelt, you'll come across a few types to choose from. Spelt flour or whole spelt includes the bran and is easily identified by the tiny specks throughout the flour. With white spelt flour, the bran has been sifted and removed for a lighter, finer texture. You can use either one for this recipe. Spelt flour can be stored in the freezer to extend its shelf life.

MAKE THE DOUGH: In a large bowl, whisk the starter and water together with a fork. Add the flours and salt. Mix to combine, and then finish by hand until a rough dough forms. Cover with a damp kitchen towel and let rest for 45 minutes to 1 hour. Replenish your starter with fresh flour and water, and store according to preference.

Meanwhile, soak the flax seeds in just enough warm water to cover while the dough is resting. Rinse and drain well before using. They will feel very sticky and gelatinous.

ADD THE FLAX SEEDS: Add the flax seeds to the bowl. Knead them into the dough, using both hands if necessary to incorporate. The dough will feel very slippery, but after about 1 minute or so, it will feel less sticky to the touch.

BULK RISE: Cover the dough with a damp towel and let rise at room temperature until double in size. This will take about 6 to 8 hours at 70°F (21°C). *Optional Step:* About 30 minutes into the bulk rise, stretch and fold the dough for added structure and height. Repeat this technique, about 2 to 3 sets, spaced 45 minutes apart (page 194).

SHAPE: Remove the dough onto a lightly oiled surface. The oil helps to combat any residual stickiness from the flax seeds. Shape the dough into a round and let rest for 5 to 10 minutes. Line an 8-inch (20-cm) bowl or proofing basket with a towel and sprinkle with flour. With floured hands, gently cup the dough and pull it toward you in a circular motion to tighten its shape. Place the dough into your bowl, seam side up.

SECOND RISE: Cover the dough and let rest until puffy but not fully risen, about 30 minutes to 1 hour.

Preheat your oven to 450°F (230°C). Cut a sheet of parchment paper to fit the size of your baking pot.

SCORE: Place the parchment over the dough and invert the bowl to release. Dust the dough with flour and rub the surface gently to coat. Poke your finger into the center of the dough, going about three-quarters of the way down. Then, make eight 3-inch (8-cm) cuts around the dough using the tip of a razor blade or knife. Use the parchment to transfer the dough into the baking pot.

BAKE: Bake the dough on the center rack for 20 minutes, covered. Remove the lid, and continue to bake for 30 minutes. Lift the bread out of the pot, and finish baking directly on the rack for the last 10 minutes. Transfer to a wire rack and cool for 1 hour before slicing.

This loaf is best enjoyed on the same day it's baked. Store at room temperature for 1 to 2 days in a plastic bag.

MIGHTY MULTIGRAIN

Makes 1 Loaf

For this recipe, you'll need a bag of Harvest Grains Blend or other 10-grain multigrain hot cereal mix to add to the dough. Both typically contain a blend of rye flakes, oats, barley, seeds, and sometimes cornmeal for a hint of mellow sweetness. These grains not only add depth of flavor but offer a brilliant textural element, too. The inside crumb will have a delightful, bouncy feel when you poke it. This sourdough is fantastic on its own or toasted, piled high with any leftovers you see fit.

About the Dough: If your grain mix contains flax or chia seeds, they will gel when soaked, making your dough stickier than usual. Lightly oil your work surface (in lieu of flouring) so it's not like prying chewing gum off the bottom of your shoe. If you happen to see lots of bubbles on the surface of this particular dough, it's an indicator of healthy fermentation.

DOUGH

50 g (¼ cup) bubbly, active starter

325 g (1⅓ cup plus 1 tsp) warm water

40 g (2 tbsp) honey

150 g (1½ cups) whole spelt flour

350 g (scant 3 cups) bread flour

9 g (1½ tsp) fine sea salt

MULTIGRAINS

70 g (½ cup) Harvest Grains Blend or 10-grain hot cereal

240 g (1 cup) hot water

Oil, for coating

A few days before baking, feed your starter until bubbly and active. Store at room temperature until ready to use.

MAKE THE DOUGH: In a large bowl, whisk the starter, water, and honey together with a fork. Add the flours and salt. Combine to form a rough, shaggy dough, and then finish by hand to fully incorporate the flour. Cover with a damp towel and let rest for 45 minutes to 1 hour. Replenish your starter with fresh flour and water, and store according to preference.

Meanwhile, soak the grains in 240 grams (1 cup) of hot water while the dough is resting. Drain well before using.

ADD THE GRAINS: Add the grains to the bowl. Knead them into the dough, using both hands as needed to incorporate, about 1 minute. The dough will feel wet and slippery but will become more manageable as you move it around.

BULK RISE: Cover the bowl with a damp towel and let rise until double in size. This will take about 6 to 8 hours at room temperature, about 70°F (21°C). *Optional Step:* About 30 minutes into the bulk rise, stretch and fold the dough for added structure and height. Repeat this technique, about 2 to 3 sets, spaced 45 minutes apart (page 194).

SHAPE: Remove the dough onto a lightly oiled work surface. Shape it into a round and let rest for 5 to 10 minutes. Meanwhile, line an 8-inch (20-cm) bowl or proofing basket with a towel. Sprinkle the inside with flour. With floured hands, gently cup the dough and pull it toward you in a circular motion to tighten its shape. Place the dough into your basket, seam side up.

SECOND RISE: Cover the dough and let rest until puffy but not fully risen, about 30 minutes to 1 hour.

Preheat your oven to 450°F (230°C). Cut a sheet of parchment paper to fit the size of your baking pot.

SCORE: Place the parchment over the dough and invert the bowl to release. Sprinkle the surface with flour and rub gently with your hands to coat. Using the tip of a small knife or razor blade, score the dough with the bird wings pattern on page 195, or any way you'd like. Use the parchment to transfer the dough into the baking pot.

BAKE: Bake the dough on the center rack for 20 minutes, covered. Remove the lid, and continue to bake for 30 minutes. Lift the bread out of the pot, and finish baking directly on the rack for the last 10 minutes. Transfer to a wire rack and cool for 1 hour before slicing.

The moisture from the grains will keep this loaf fresh for 1 to 2 days. Store at room temperature in a plastic bag.

LIGHT RYE

Makes 1 Loaf

Confession: Initially, I assumed that rye in sourdough would make everything taste like pastrami sandwiches. You know that classic rye bread taste? Don't get me wrong—pastrami sandwiches are tasty. But after a few experiments, I quickly learned that rye flour is quite mild on its own. It's everything else going on in rye bread, caraway seeds included, that defines its characteristic taste. Rye pairs perfectly with sourdough, and I encourage you to give it a go. Try this loaf warm or toasted with a slice of cheddar and a dab of apricot jam.

About the Dough: This recipe uses white or light rye, which is different than whole rye flour. It's lighter in color and not as coarse in texture. Rye is also low in gluten, so here it's combined with bread flour for structure and height. This dough tends to ferment quickly, so keep your eye on it as it begins to rise.

50 g (¼ cup) bubbly, active starter

365 g (1½ cups plus 1 tsp) warm water

20 g (1 tbsp) honey

106 g (1 cup) white rye flour

400 g (3⅓ cups) bread flour

9 g (1½ tsp) fine sea salt

A few days before baking, feed your starter until bubbly and active. Store at room temperature until ready to use.

MAKE THE DOUGH: In a large bowl, whisk the starter, water, and honey together with a fork. Add the flours and salt. Mix to combine, then finish by hand to form a rough dough. Cover with a damp towel and let rest for 30 minutes. Replenish your starter with fresh flour and water, and store according to preference.

After the dough has rested, work it into a fairly smooth ball, about 15 seconds.

BULK RISE: Cover the bowl with a damp towel and let rise at room temperature until double in size. This will take about 6 to 8 hours at room temperature, about 70°F (21°C). *Optional Step:* About 30 minutes into the bulk rise, stretch and fold the dough for added structure and height. Repeat this technique, about 2 to 3 sets, spaced 45 minutes apart (page 194).

SHAPE: Remove the dough onto a well-floured work surface. Shape the dough into a round or oval and let rest for 5 to 10 minutes. Line an 8-inch (20-cm) bowl or 10-inch (25-cm) oval proofing basket with a towel and sprinkle with flour. With floured hands, gently cup the dough and tighten to your desired shape. Place the dough into your proofing vessel, seam side up.

SECOND RISE: Cover the dough and let rest until puffy but not fully risen, about 30 to 45 minutes, depending on temperature. Preheat your oven to 450°F (230°C). Cut a sheet of parchment paper to fit the size of your baking pot.

SCORE: Place the parchment over the dough and invert the proofing vessel to release. Sprinkle the dough with flour and rub gently to coat. Choose a scoring pattern from page 195 or, if you prefer, make one long cut down the length of the loaf. Then use the parchment to transfer the dough into the baking pot.

BAKE: Bake the dough on the center rack for 20 minutes, covered. Remove the lid, and continue to bake for 30 minutes. Lift the bread out of the pot, and finish baking directly on the rack for the last 10 minutes. Transfer to a wire rack and cool for 1 hour before slicing.

This loaf will stay fresh up to 1 day stored at room temperature in a plastic bag.

TOASTED SUNFLOWER
Makes 1 Loaf

One of my favorites in this chapter, this blend of earthy flours creates a harmonious sourdough that will undoubtedly beckon you, slice after slice. It's an excellent loaf for wholesome sandwiches and to enjoy with balsamic-dressed leafy green salads. The toasted sunflower seeds, although they are pesky and bounce all over the floor, take the crust to the next level.

About the Dough: This dough was born purely out of experimentation. You'll notice it has a unique texture, too, slightly gritty from the semolina flour and little muddy from the rye. After a long initial rest, it will absorb all the water it needs to soften the texture and make the dough easier to shape.

50 g (¼ cup) bubbly, active starter

365 g (1½ cups plus 1 tsp) warm water

100 g (⅔ cup) semolina flour

100 g (¾ cup plus 1 tbsp) white whole wheat flour

50 g (½ cup) white rye flour

300 g (2½ cups) bread flour

9 g (1½ tsp) fine sea salt

180 g (1½ cups) sunflower seeds, for coating

A few days before baking, feed your starter until bubbly and active. Store at room temperature until ready to use.

MAKE THE DOUGH: In a large bowl, whisk the starter and water together with a fork. Add the flours and salt. Combine to form a rough dough, then finish mixing by hand until the flour is fully absorbed. Cover with a damp towel and let rest for 45 minutes to 1 hour. Meanwhile, replenish your starter with fresh flour and water, and store according to preference.

After the dough has rested, work it into a fairly smooth ball, about 15 to 20 seconds.

BULK RISE: Cover the bowl with a damp towel and let rise at room temperature until double in size. This will take about 6 to 8 hours at 70°F (21°C). *Optional Step:* About 30 minutes into the bulk rise, stretch and fold the dough for added structure and height. Repeat this technique, about 2 to 3 sets, spaced 45 minutes apart (page 194).

SHAPE THE DOUGH AND COAT WITH SEEDS: Remove the dough onto a floured work surface. Shape it into an oval and let rest for 5 to 10 minutes. Meanwhile, line a 10-inch (25-cm) oval proofing basket with a towel and set aside. Spread the sunflower seeds on a damp kitchen towel.

With floured hands, gently cup the dough and pull it toward you to tighten its shape. Lightly brush the surface and sides of the dough with water. Using a bench scraper, place the dough onto the seeds, wet side down. Lift both sides of the towel and rock it back and forth to coat the dough. Place the dough into your basket, seam side up.

SECOND RISE: Cover the dough and let rest until puffy but not fully risen, about 30 minutes to 1 hour.

Preheat your oven to 450°F (230°C). Cut a sheet of parchment paper to fit the size of your baking pot.

SCORE: Place the parchment over the dough and invert the basket to release. Score the dough straight down the length of the loaf, using the tip of a sharp paring knife or razor blade. Use the parchment to transfer the dough into the baking pot.

BAKE: Bake the dough on the center rack for 20 minutes, covered. Remove the lid, and continue to bake for 40 minutes. When finished, transfer the loaf to a wire rack. Cool for 1 hour before slicing.

This loaf will stay fresh up to 1 day in a plastic bag, stored at room temperature.

GOLDEN SESAME SEMOLINA

Makes 1 Loaf

Semolina is a beautiful, pale yellow flour made from durum wheat. It's coarser than regular flour, which you'll notice right away when you rub it between your fingers. It feels like fine sand. The flavor of semolina is not very pronounced, but its versatility extends into cakes, crackers, rolls, and even pizza. You'll love the velvety, soft texture it adds to this sourdough, as well as its gorgeous golden color.

About the Dough: When combined with water, semolina flour will make the dough feel very gritty at first. Intuitively, you'll want to add more bread flour to even out the texture, but resist the urge, or it will become too dry. After resting, the dough will become much softer and pleasing to work with.

50 g (¼ cup) bubbly, active starter

350 g (1⅓ cups plus 2 tbsp) warm water

250 g (1½ cups) semolina flour

275 g (about 2¼ cups) bread flour

9 g (1½ tsp) fine sea salt

120 g (¾ cup) sesame seeds, for coating

A few days before baking, feed your starter until bubbly and active. Store at room temperature until ready to use.

MAKE THE DOUGH: In a large bowl, whisk the starter and water together with a fork. Add the flours and salt. Mix to combine, then finish by hand until the flour is fully absorbed. Cover with a damp towel and let rest for 45 minutes to 1 hour. Replenish your starter with fresh flour and water, and store according to preference.

After the dough has rested, work the mass into a fairly smooth ball, about 15 to 20 seconds. The dough will feel much softer at this stage.

BULK RISE: Cover the bowl with a damp towel and let rise at room temperature, 70°F (21°C), until double in size, about 6 to 8 hours. *Optional Step:* About 30 minutes into the bulk rise, stretch and fold the dough for added structure and height. Repeat this technique, about 2 to 3 sets, spaced 45 minutes apart (page 194).

SHAPE THE DOUGH AND COAT WITH SEEDS: Remove the dough onto a lightly floured work surface. Shape it into a round and let rest for 5 to 10 minutes. Meanwhile, line an 8-inch (20-cm) bowl or proofing basket with a towel. Spread the sesame seeds on a damp kitchen towel.

With floured hands, gently cup the dough and pull it toward you in a circular motion to tighten its shape. Then lightly brush the surface and sides of the dough with water. Using a bench scraper, place the dough onto the seeds, wet side down. Lift both sides of the towel and rock it back and forth to coat the dough. Place the dough into your bowl, seam side up.

SECOND RISE: Cover the dough and let rest until puffy but not fully risen, about 30 minutes to 1 hour.

Preheat your oven to 450°F (230°C). Cut a sheet of parchment paper to fit the size of your baking pot.

SCORE: Place the parchment over the dough and invert the bowl to release. Make three 4-inch (10-cm) long cuts in the shape of a triangle with a small serrated knife or a razor blade. Use the parchment to transfer the dough into the baking pot.

BAKE: Bake the dough on the center rack for 20 minutes, covered. Remove the lid, and continue to bake for 40 minutes. Transfer the loaf to a wire rack and cool for 1 hour before slicing.

To maximize freshness, store at room temperature in a plastic bag, up to 1 day.

RUSTIC PUMPERNICKEL

Makes 1 Loaf

This sourdough is rich, slightly sweet, and boasts a beautiful toffee color. It uses pumpernickel flour, also known as whole rye, which is made from coarsely ground rye berries. Once baked, the crust becomes extra crunchy with a hearty, fennel-kissed crumb. I love grilled pumpernickel sandwiches with turkey, melted Swiss, and coleslaw. Or try a few slices with my feel-good Weeknight Tuscan Ribollita soup (page 167).

About the Dough: Because pumpernickel flour lacks sufficient gluten, this dough will feel very stiff, similar to wet mud when mixed. Sounds appetizing, doesn't it? Add the oil after the dough has rested. This was initially my human error, but it turned out to be one of those happy mistakes that makes better bread. Place this dough inside a well-floured proofing basket to create whimsical powdered lines on the outside crust.

50 g (¼ cup) bubbly, active starter

365 g (1½ cups plus 1 tsp) warm water

40 g (2 tbsp) unsulphured molasses

120 g (1 cup) pumpernickel flour

380 g (about 3¼ cups) bread flour

9 g (1½ tsp) fine sea salt

30 g (2 tbsp) oil

5 g (1 tbsp) fennel seeds, optional

A few days before baking, feed your starter until bubbly and active. Store at room temperature until ready to use.

MAKE THE DOUGH: In a large bowl, whisk the starter, water, and molasses together with a fork. Add the flours and salt. Combine until a thick, dense dough forms and then finish by hand until the flour is absorbed. Cover with a damp towel and let rest for 45 minutes to 1 hour. Meanwhile, replenish your starter with fresh flour and water, and store according to preference.

After the dough has rested, add the oil and fennel seeds, if using, to the bowl. Gently knead to incorporate or until the oil is well absorbed. The dough will feel much softer and not as stiff as it was earlier.

BULK RISE: Cover the bowl with a damp towel and let rise at room temperature until double in size, about 8 to 10 hours at 70°F (21°C).

SHAPE: Remove the dough out onto a lightly floured surface. Shape into a round and let rest for 5 to 10 minutes. Meanwhile, dust an 8-inch (20-cm) proofing basket with flour. With floured hands, gently cup the dough and pull it toward you in a circular motion to tighten its shape. Place the dough into your basket, seam side up.

SECOND RISE: Cover the dough and let rest until puffy, but not double in size, about 1½ to 2 hours, depending on temperature.

Preheat your oven to 450°F (230°C). Cut a sheet of parchment paper to fit the size of your baking pot.

SCORE: Place the parchment over the dough and invert the basket to release. Using the tip of a small knife or razor blade, make four shallow 4-inch (10-cm) long cuts at 3, 6, 9, and 12 o'clock around the dough. Then, make four leaf-shaped cuts in between. Use the parchment to transfer the dough into the baking pot.

BAKE: Bake the dough, covered, on the center rack for 20 minutes. Remove the lid, and continue to bake for 40 minutes. If the loaf starts to brown too quickly because of the sugars in the molasses, loosely tent with foil. Transfer to a wire rack and cool for 1 hour before slicing

This sourdough will last for 1 to 2 days stored at room temperature in a plastic bag.

FOCACCIA, ROLLS, and EVERYTHING ELSE

Focaccia is a busy bread baker's dream. The dough is practically hands-off and can be worked into any weeknight schedule in a variety of ways. I find myself making the Basic No-Knead Focaccia (page 92) at least once a week for quick and easy pizzas and to serve with soup. The texture is light, crispy, and addicting. Also included are several recipes for sourdough rolls, soft breadsticks, and an updated twist on the baguette. All different, but equally delicious, these sourdoughs share two things in common: They are easy to make and guaranteed to please a crowd.

BASIC NO-KNEAD FOCACCIA

Makes 1 Large Focaccia

See, the thing is, you haven't experienced focaccia until you've tried real homemade focaccia. I'm not talking about those pale, underwhelming doughy slabs served at chain restaurants. I'm talking about sourdough focaccia that's generously drizzled with olive oil and baked to perfection with a crust so crisp it's practically fried. The corner pieces are killer. Real focaccia, naturally leavened and served warm, is one of life's greatest pleasures.

About the Dough: Focaccia doesn't require much. There's no kneading. No shaping. No scoring. Let it rise overnight, anywhere from 12 to 18 hours. Then let the dough hang out in a well-oiled pan before dimpling all over with your fingertips. I like to make the dough at night to bake in the morning. Before serving, I'll reheat it in a low oven to wow my guests (or myself) during the week.

Note: Use cool water in the dough, in lieu of warm, to control the long overnight rise. This helps to avoid overproofed or collapsed dough in the morning.

DOUGH

50 g (¼ cup) bubbly, active starter

375 g (1½ cups plus 1 tbsp) cool water

20 g (1 tbsp) honey

500 g (4 cups plus 2 tbsp) all-purpose flour

9 g (1½ tsp) fine sea salt

45 g (3 tbsp) olive oil, for coating the pan

OPTIONAL TOPPINGS

Rosemary sprigs, leaves picked

Garlic cloves, with their papery shells intact

Flaky salt

A few days before baking, feed your starter until bubbly and active. Store at room temperature until ready to use.

MAKE THE DOUGH: In the evening, whisk the starter, water, and honey together in a large bowl with a fork. Add the flour and salt. Mix to combine, then finish by hand to fully incorporate the flour. The dough will be very sticky. Replenish your starter with fresh flour and water, and store according to preference.

BULK RISE: Cover the bowl with a damp towel and let rise overnight at room temperature, 70°F (21°C), about 12 to 18 hours. The dough will double in size (or more) and look stringy when removed from the bowl. There might be a few bubbles on the surface as well.

SECOND RISE: In the morning, pour the olive oil onto a rimmed sheet pan. Use your hands to evenly coat the bottom and sides. Remove the dough onto the sheet pan, and then flip it over so that both sides are coated in the oil. You don't need to pull or stretch the dough at this time. It will look like a blob. Cover and let rest for about 1½ to 2 hours, or until very puffy.

Preheat your oven to 425°F (220°C).

ASSEMBLE THE FOCACCIA: Gently stretch the dough into a rustic rectangular or oval shape, about 14 × 9 inches (36 × 23 cm) or larger. The dough won't reach all of the way to the corners and sides of the pan. Use your fingertips to dimple the dough, pressing straight through to the bottom of the pan. If using, press the rosemary leaves and garlic cloves into the dough and sprinkle with flaky salt.

BAKE: Bake the focaccia for 25 to 30 minutes or until crisp and golden brown. Remove from the oven, and cool before cutting into wedges using a pizza wheel or large knife. Serve warm.

This focaccia will last up to 2 days, wrapped in foil at room temperature. For the best texture, reheat gently to serve.

TIPS: Don't skimp on the amount of oil for coating the pan. It not only prevents sticking but also helps to achieve an authentic, crispy crust. Use regular olive oil instead of extra virgin, which has a tendency to burn quickly due to its low smoke point. You can also bake this focaccia in a 9 × 13-inch (23 × 33-cm) baking pan for 30 minutes at 425°F (220°C).

NO-KNEAD TOMATO BASIL FOCACCIA

Makes 1 Large Focaccia

Marinating tomatoes in silky olive oil and adding crushed fennel seeds are the secrets to making this variation on the Basic No-Knead Focaccia (page 92) extra flavorful. When you halve the tomatoes, the intense heat during baking concentrates their flavor, making them blistered and extra sweet. I love serving this sourdough with fresh mozzarella or burrata and a drizzle of thick, aged balsamic vinegar.

About the Dough: This focaccia is baked in a rectangle pan which hugs the dough as it bakes, creating an incredible crust along the edges. Its shape lends itself well for sandwiches, too; simply halve the bread horizontally, stack with toppings, and grill on a panini press for a delicious toasted treat.

1 recipe Basic No-Knead Focaccia (page 92)

45 g (3 tbsp) olive oil, for coating the pan

MARINATED TOMATOES

270 g (2 cups) whole grape tomatoes

2 g (1 tsp) fennel seeds or Herbes de Provence

Pinch of sugar

15 g (1 tbsp) olive oil

Salt and freshly ground black pepper

Fresh basil leaves, for serving

A few days before baking, feed your starter until bubbly and active. Store at room temperature until ready to use.

MAKE THE DOUGH: Follow the instructions for making the Basic No-Knead Focaccia on page 92. When the bulk rise is complete, proceed to the next step.

SECOND RISE: Pour the olive oil into a 9 × 13-inch (23 × 33-cm) baking pan. Use your hands to evenly coat the bottom and sides. Remove the dough into the pan, and then flip it over so that both sides are coated in the oil. Cover and let rest for about 1½ to 2 hours, or until very puffy.

MARINATE THE TOMATOES: While the dough is resting, halve the grape tomatoes and toss them into a shallow bowl. Crush the fennel seeds by running your knife through them just a few times. Add the fennel seeds to the bowl with a pinch of sugar. Drizzle with olive oil and season with salt and pepper. Toss gently and let the flavors marinate until the focaccia is ready to bake.

Preheat your oven to 425°F (220°C).

ASSEMBLE THE FOCACCIA: Gently stretch the dough to reach the corner and sides of the pan. Spoon the tomatoes over the top, reserving the juice in the bowl. Gently dimple the dough all over, pressing the tomatoes into the dough as you go.

BAKE: Bake for 30 minutes or until the focaccia is beautifully crisp and the tomatoes are deep red and blistered. Serve warm, cut into wedges, with fresh basil leaves. This focaccia is best enjoyed on the day it's made.

STUFFED CROQUE MONSIEUR FOCACCIA WITH RICOTTA *and* SWISS

Makes 1 Large Focaccia

Have you ever tried a croque monsieur? It's a crisp, buttery, fried ham and cheese sandwich popular in French bistros. Here, thin slices of ham and Swiss are layered between focaccia dough for the ultimate stuffed sourdough sandwich. The surface is painted with piquant Dijon mustard and dolloped generously with creamy ricotta to finish. Serve warm, and invite everyone you know to gather round for a thick-cut wedge straight from the oven. This, my friends, is sourdough heaven.

About the Dough: The trick to making stuffed focaccia is all in the sandwich-style shaping. For best results, as you layer the dough, make sure to stretch and dimple as evenly as you can. This will avoid any large, cavernous air pockets and promote even cooking throughout the dough.

DOUGH

50 g (¼ cup) bubbly, active starter

400 g (1⅔ cups) cool water

20 g (1 tbsp) honey

450 g (3¾ cups) all-purpose flour

50 g (⅓ cup plus 1 tbsp) whole wheat flour

9 g (1½ tsp) fine sea salt

45 g (3 tbsp) olive oil, divided, for coating

TOPPINGS

8 slices of Swiss cheese, divided

8 slices of good-quality ham or prosciutto, divided

20 g (1 tbsp) Dijon mustard

250 g (2 cups) whole milk ricotta

A few days before baking, feed your starter until bubbly and active. Store at room temperature until ready to use.

MAKE THE DOUGH: In the evening, whisk the starter, water, and honey together in a large bowl with a fork. Add the flours and salt. Mix to combine, then finish by hand to form a rough, shaggy dough. Replenish your starter with fresh flour and water, and store according to preference.

BULK RISE: Cover the bowl with a damp towel and let rise overnight at room temperature, 70°F (21°C), about 12 to 18 hours. The dough is ready when it has doubled or tripled in size.

DIVIDE: Remove the dough onto a lightly floured work surface. Divide the dough in half using a wet knife or bench scraper. Coat a rimmed sheet pan with 30 grams (2 tbsp) of olive oil. Pour the remaining 15 grams (1 tbsp) onto a large plate—no need for an additional sheet pan. Place one piece of dough on the sheet pan and the other on the plate.

SECOND RISE: Cover each piece of dough with a damp towel. Let rest for about 1 to 2 hours or until noticeably puffy.

Preheat your oven to 425°F (220°C).

ASSEMBLE THE FOCACCIA: Working with the dough on the sheet pan, gently stretch into a large rectangular shape, about 14 × 9 inches (36 × 23 cm) or larger. Evenly arrange 4 slices of Swiss and 4 slices of ham on top. Lift and stretch the remaining piece of dough and place it over the toppings to create a sandwich. Stretch and dimple the surface, docking the sides with your fingertips to seal the dough and to evenly distribute the weight.

Brush the dough generously with Dijon mustard. Tear the remaining slices of Swiss and ham and arrange over the top. Dimple the toppings into the dough so they do not pop out when baked. Dollop with the ricotta cheese.

BAKE: Bake the focaccia for 30 to 40 minutes, or until deep golden brown. The cheese will bubble, the ham will get slightly crisp, and the ricotta will become warm and creamy. It will smell amazing. Cut into wedges or squares. Serve warm.

This focaccia will last up to 2 days, wrapped in foil at room temperature. Reheat to serve or enjoy at room temperature.

NO-KNEAD FOCACCIA PIZZA WITH PESTO and FONTINA

Makes 1 Large Focaccia

Focaccia pizzas are a home cook's best kept secret. As long as you've got some dough, they are quick to put together any night of the week. For this focaccia pizza, you'll find fresh basil pesto spread on top, and it's smothered in creamy fontina cheese to finish. The crust bakes up golden and crunchy, while the inside is light and airy. I guarantee you'll give your local pizzeria a run for their money. Many napkins are required for this one.

About the Dough: For extra flavor, this focaccia has a generous dollop of basil pesto added to the dough. It will smell incredible as it begins to rise.

DOUGH

50 g (¼ cup) bubbly, active starter

400 g (1⅔ cups) cool water

18 g (1 heaped tbsp) basil pesto

500 g (4 cups plus 2 tbsp) all-purpose flour

5 g (1 tsp) fine sea salt

45 g (3 tbsp) olive oil, for coating

PESTO AND CHEESE TOPPING

120 to 160 g (½ to ⅔ cup) basil pesto

125 g (2 lightly packed cups) shredded fontina cheese

Sprinkle of red pepper flakes

Parmesan cheese, to taste

Handful of fresh basil leaves

A few days before baking, feed your starter until bubbly and active. Store at room temperature until ready to use.

MAKE THE DOUGH: In the evening, whisk the starter, water, and pesto together in a large bowl with a fork. Add the flour and salt. Mix to combine, then finish by hand until no lumps of flour remain. Replenish your starter with fresh flour and water, and store according to preference.

BULK RISE: Cover the dough with a damp towel and let rise overnight at room temperature, 70°F (21°C), about 12 to 18 hours. The dough will double in size (or more) and look stringy when removed from the bowl.

SECOND RISE: Pour the olive oil onto a rimmed sheet pan, and rub the bottom and sides with your hands. Coax the dough onto the sheet pan, then flip it over so that both sides are coated in the oil. Cover and let rest for about 1½ to 2 hours, or until very puffy.

Preheat your oven to 425°F (220°C).

ASSEMBLE THE FOCACCIA: Gently dimple the surface of the dough, stretching and rounding the sides into a large, rustic oval shape. The size should be about 14 × 9 inches (36 × 23 cm). Spread the pesto over the dough, smoothing it out with the back of a spoon. Hold off on adding the cheese for now.

BAKE: Bake the focaccia for 25 minutes. Remove from the oven and sprinkle the fontina cheese over the top. Bake for an additional 5 to 7 minutes or until the cheese is bubbling and melted. Before serving, sprinkle with red pepper flakes, Parmesan cheese, and extra pesto to taste. Scatter the fresh basil leaves on top. Cut into slices and serve warm. This focaccia is best enjoyed on the day it's made.

NO-KNEAD CHOCOLATE CHUNK FOCACCIA WITH CREAM CHEESE *and* NUTELLA

Makes 1 Skillet Focaccia

My love for chocolate sourdough runs deep, and I could probably pen and eat a whole book on the subject. Focaccia is no exception. This decadent chocolate focaccia is topped with cream cheese and chocolate hazelnut spread, which melt slowly into the dough once baked. My advice? Tear off a chunk and dunk it into the warm center. For an added bonus, this focaccia is baked in melted butter.

About the Dough: This dough will feel extremely stiff after mixing due to the cocoa powder. Additional water softens the dough, and once it finishes rising, it will become beautiful and supple. For best results, make sure to thoroughly combine the flour and cocoa powder first, before adding the rest of the ingredients. This will avoid zebra stripes running through your dough.

DOUGH

500 g (4 cups plus 2 tbsp) all-purpose flour

20 g (¼ cup) cocoa powder

5 g (1 tsp) fine sea salt

50 g (¼ cup) bubbly, active starter

400 g (1⅔ cups) cool water

20 g (1 tbsp) honey

5 g (1 tsp) pure vanilla extract

90 g (½ cup) semi-sweet chocolate chips, plus extra as needed

70 g (5 tbsp) unsalted butter, melted

TOPPINGS

2 large dollops of Nutella, or chocolate hazelnut spread

2 large dollops of cream cheese

Small handful of raspberries, pomegranate seeds, and strawberries

Powdered sugar, to serve

A few days before baking, feed your starter until bubbly and active. Store at room temperature until ready to use.

MAKE THE DOUGH: In the evening, whisk the flour, cocoa powder, and salt together in a large bowl with a fork. Add the starter, water, honey, and vanilla. Mix to combine, then finish by hand to form a rough and shaggy dough. Cover the bowl and let rest for 45 minutes to 1 hour. Meanwhile, replenish your starter with fresh flour and water, and store according to preference.

After the dough has rested, add the chocolate chips to the bowl. Gently knead to incorporate, about 1 minute.

BULK RISE: Cover the bowl with a damp towel and let rise overnight at room temperature, 70°F (21°C), about 12 to 18 hours.

SECOND RISE: Melt the butter in a small saucepan over low heat, or in the microwave. Pour the butter into a 10-inch (25-cm) cast iron skillet and swirl to coat. Cool for a few minutes before adding the dough. Remove the dough into the skillet, and then flip it over to coat both sides in the melted butter. Cover and let rest for about 1 hour or more, until very puffy. The butter may solidify during this stage, depending on the room temperature.

Preheat your oven to 425°F (220°C).

ASSEMBLE THE FOCACCIA: Gently dimple and stretch the dough to reach the sides of the skillet. Sprinkle with a small handful of extra chocolate chips, pressing them into the dough as you go.

BAKE: Bake the focaccia for 35 to 40 minutes. Remove from the oven and cool for 10 minutes. Spread some of the Nutella over the top, and then dollop the center with cream cheese. When ready to serve, top with raspberries, pomegranate seeds, and strawberries. Sprinkle generously with powdered sugar. Enjoy while still warm.

FOCACCIA DI RECCO

Makes 2 Crispy Focaccia Rounds

Yes, I know. This looks more like a quesadilla than your typical focaccia. But this is Ligurian-style focaccia, best described as a crispy, paper-thin flatbread stuffed with creamy, melted cheese. It's irresistible. Traditionally, this focaccia is made with Stracchino, a soft, delicate cow's milk cheese. Stracchino can be challenging to find, so as an alternative, I've made it with mascarpone and fontina for an updated twist.

About the Dough: For this particular recipe, it's all about how you stretch the dough. You'll do this pizzeria-style minus the air toss, letting the natural weight of the dough do the work for you. The cheese is dolloped on top, covered with another sheet of dough, and then baked to crispy perfection. You'll need the base of two 10-inch (25-cm) springform pans or a small pizza pan to bake the focaccia.

DOUGH

75 g (heaped ⅓ cup) bubbly, active starter

220 g (scant 1 cup) warm water

15 g (1 tbsp) olive oil, plus more for brushing

400 g (3⅓ cups) bread flour

9 g (1½ tsp) fine sea salt

FILLING

70 g (⅓ cup) mascarpone cheese

30 g (heaped ½ cup) grated fontina cheese

Salt and freshly ground black pepper, to taste

Small handful of watercress or arugula

A few days before baking, feed your starter until bubbly and active. Store at room temperature until ready to use.

TIP: You can also stuff this focaccia with cured meat, like prosciutto or hot soppressata, or thin slices of fried eggplant and broccoli rabe.

MAKE THE DOUGH: In a medium bowl, whisk the starter, water, and olive oil together with a fork. Add the flour and salt. Combine to form a rough dough, then finish mixing by hand to fully incorporate the flour. Cover with a damp towel and let rest for 1 to 2 hours. The dough doesn't need to rise much at this stage, but the longer it rests, the easier it will be to roll and stretch.

Replenish your starter with fresh flour and water, and store it according to preference.

CHEESE FILLING: Add the mascarpone and grated fontina to a small bowl. Season lightly with salt and pepper, and mash with a fork to combine. Refrigerate the mixture until ready to use.

ROLL AND SHAPE: Brush the bottom of two 10-inch (25-cm) springform pans with olive oil and set aside.

Remove the dough onto a lightly floured work surface. Divide into 4 equal pieces. (It's not necessary to weigh the dough.) Roll one piece into an 8-inch (20-cm) circle. Lift the dough and gently stretch the edges while turning in a circular motion to create a large round, about 1 minute.

Once the dough becomes noticeably larger, make a fist with one hand and drape the dough over the top. Sneak your other hand underneath. Using both hands, continue to turn the dough, using your knuckles to stretch and pull the surface. The dough is ready when you have created a large round that's tissue-paper thin. Hold it up in front of a window to double check; you should be able to see through to the other side. *Note:* If there's any resistance or if you need to take a break, drape the dough over the back of a chair and let rest for 5 minutes.

ASSEMBLE THE FOCACCIA: Drape the dough over the oiled pan, letting the excess hang over the sides. Dollop the surface with half of the cold cheese mixture. Roll and stretch a second piece of dough and drape it over the cheese. It will look like a pie. Let rest for 10 minutes, and then trim the excess dough around the sides. Meanwhile, roll, shape, and assemble the remaining 2 pieces of dough with the cheese.

Preheat your oven to 500°F (260°C).

BAKE: Brush the focaccias with olive oil and sprinkle with salt. Make a few slits in the top layer for the steam to escape. Bake for 7 to 8 minutes. The focaccias will puff up and become golden and crisp when ready. Cool for 1 to 2 minutes before cutting into wedges, if you can wait that long!

Top with tangled watercress or arugula for a pop of fresh green color to serve.

SOFT SHARE *and* TEAR ROLLS
Makes 12 Soft Rolls

These are the most talked-about rolls in our house. Everyone goes crazy for them. They're incredibly soft and slightly sweet, with just a touch of butter for richness. They are delicious plain, but the kids love to gobble them up with butter and jam. The dough is incredibly versatile, too, and can be shaped into delicious sandwich rolls.

About the Dough: To really nail that soft, shreddable, inside crumb, you'll need a stand mixer to incorporate air into the dough. Due to the richness of the butter and eggs, it requires additional strength in order to rise, so consider the mixer your secret ingredient. These rolls can be shaped and refrigerated overnight to deepen the flavor.

DOUGH
240 g (1 cup) milk, whole or 2%

60 g (¼ cup) water

28 g (2 tbsp) unsalted butter, cubed, plus more for coating

1 large egg

200 g (1 cup) bubbly, active starter

24 g (2 tbsp) sugar

450 g (3¾ cups) bread flour

5 g (1 tsp) fine sea salt

EGG WASH
1 large egg

Splash of water

A few days before baking, feed your starter until bubbly and active. Store at room temperature until ready to use.

SANDWICH AND BURGER ROLL VARIATION: Shape
the dough into 8 balls, about 125 grams (4½ oz) each. Brush the tops with egg wash and pat down slightly so they're not so plump (the dough will pop back up as they bake). Bake at 400°F (200°C) for 25 minutes or until golden brown.

MAKE THE DOUGH: In a small saucepan, warm the milk, water, and butter over low heat or in the microwave. Cool slightly before adding to the dough.

Meanwhile, add 1 egg, starter, and sugar to the bowl of a stand mixer fitted with the paddle attachment. Mix on low speed to combine. Gradually add the warm milk mixture, followed by the flour and salt. Continue to mix until a wet and sticky dough forms, about 1 to 2 minutes. The texture will look very similar to cake batter. When finished, scrape down the sides of the bowl. Cover and let rest for 30 minutes. Replenish your starter with fresh flour and water, and store according to preference.

After the dough has rested, switch to the dough hook and knead on medium-low speed, about 6 to 8 minutes. The dough will not come together in a ball but will look shiny and smooth when ready. Scrape down the sides of the bowl once more.

BULK RISE: Transfer the dough to a new bowl lightly coated in butter. Cover the dough and find a warm spot for it to rise. This could be near a heater, on top of the fridge, or even in a cabinet. Let it rest until double in size, about 6 to 8 hours, depending on temperature.

SHAPE: Lightly coat a 9 × 13-inch (23 × 33-cm) baking pan with butter.

Remove the dough onto a lightly floured surface. With floured fingertips, gently flatten into a rectangle. Cut the dough into 12 pieces, about 85 grams (3 oz) each, with a floured knife or bench scraper. Gather the ends, flip the dough over, and roll each piece into a ball. Place into your pan, 3 pieces across and 4 down.

SECOND RISE: Cover the pan with a damp towel and let rest for 1 hour or more, depending on temperature. The dough should look puffy, but not fully risen, when ready. Alternatively, cover the dough with lightly oiled plastic wrap and chill overnight, up to 8 hours. Return to room temperature before baking, about 1 hour.

Preheat your oven to 400°F (200°C). Combine the remaining egg with a splash of water. Brush the tops of the dough for a shiny finish.

BAKE: Bake the rolls on the center rack for about 35 to 40 minutes. The rolls will be fully risen and rich golden brown when finished. Serve warm or at room temperature, family-style, to share and tear.

Soft rolls will last up to 2 to 3 days. Store in a plastic bag at room temperature to maximize freshness.

EASY BREAD BASKET ROLLS
Makes 10 to 12 Small Rolls

These rolls are fantastic for just about anything: mini sandwiches, soup, snacking, to serve with dinner—you name it. The dough is lightly sweet and boasts a nice yeasty quality when milk is added to it. You'll find yourself eating them warm, straight out of the oven.

About the Dough: This is a wonderful dough to work with, as it's firm and easy to shape. Use both all-purpose flour and bread flour to achieve a soft, chewy texture. For timing, you can chill the bulk dough once it has fully risen and bake when you have the time. Chilled dough is very convenient for spontaneous sourdough bakes.

100 g (½ cup) bubbly, active starter

240 g (1 cup) warm water

80 g (⅓ cup) warm milk, whole or 2%

24 g (2 tbsp) sugar

360 g (3 cups) bread flour

140 g (1 cup plus 2 tbsp) all-purpose flour

9 g (1½ tsp) fine sea salt

Cornmeal or semolina flour, for dusting

A few days before baking, feed your starter until bubbly and active. Store at room temperature until ready to use.

MAKE THE DOUGH: In a large bowl, whisk the starter, water, milk, and sugar together with a fork. Add the flours and salt. Mix to combine, then finish by hand until the flour is fully absorbed. Cover with a damp towel and let rest for 30 minutes. Meanwhile, replenish your starter with fresh flour and water, and store according to preference.

After the dough has rested, work the mass into a semi-smooth ball, about 15 to 20 seconds.

BULK RISE: Cover the bowl with a damp towel and let rise until double in size, about 8 to 10 hours at room temperature, 70°F (21°C). Alternatively, once fully risen, cover the dough with lightly oiled plastic wrap and chill overnight.

SHAPE: Line a sheet pan with parchment paper and dust with cornmeal. Set aside. Remove the dough onto a lightly floured surface and gently flatten into a rectangle. Cut the dough into 12 equal pieces, about 80 grams (2¾ oz) each, with a floured knife or bench scraper. Gather the ends, flip the dough over, and roll each piece into a ball. Place onto your sheet pan, 3 pieces across and 4 down.

SECOND RISE: Cover the dough and let rest for about 1 hour or until noticeable puffy. If you're working with chilled dough, allow for more time, depending on temperature.

Preheat your oven to 400°F (200°C).

SCORE THE DOUGH: Lightly dust the rolls with cornmeal. Using the tip of a small knife or razor blade, score the top of each roll, about 1½ inches (4 cm) long, straight down the center.

BAKE: Bake the rolls on the center rack for about 25 to 30 minutes. Their color will go from whitish blonde to golden when finished. Cool directly on the sheet pan and serve warm.

These rolls will last up to 1 day, stored at room temperature in a plastic bag.

BLISTERED ASIAGO ROLLS WITH SWEET APPLES *and* ROSEMARY

Makes 12 Rolls

Undeniably flavorful with a soft and chewy interior, these scrumptious rolls are a must-make. Enjoy them solo or with a bowl of velvety pumpkin soup. The best part is the cheese! Mounds of Asiago melt into golden, blistered shells that wrap around sweet apples and rosemary. Just wait until you try one. These rolls spark excellent conversation, too, if you'd like to present them at your next holiday gathering.

About the Dough: This dough holds up well when chilled. Once fully risen, you can chill the bulk dough in the fridge overnight. This way, you can shape and bake the rolls when the mood strikes, perhaps right before dinner.

DOUGH

50 g (¼ cup) bubbly, active starter

350 g (1⅓ cups plus 2 tbsp) warm water

500 g (4 cups plus 2 tbsp) bread flour

9 g (1½ tsp) fine sea salt

FILLINGS

80 g (¾ cups) chopped, dried apple rings

1 g (2 tsp) chopped rosemary

220 g (½ lb) wedge of Asiago or white cheddar cheese, grated

A few days before baking, feed your starter until bubbly and active. Store at room temperature until ready to use.

TIP: It's best to use chewy, dried apples for this recipe. Although fresh apples will work, too, you'll have to sauté them first to reduce their natural moisture content. Using dried apples eliminates this step. They also hold their shape much better and have a more concentrated apple flavor.

MAKE THE DOUGH: In a large bowl, whisk the starter and water together with a fork. Add the flour and salt. Combine to form a rough dough, finishing by hand to incorporate all of the flour. Cover with a damp towel and let rest for 30 to 45 minutes. Replenish your starter with fresh flour and water, and store according to preference.

Meanwhile, soak the apples in a bowl of warm water until the dough has finished resting. Drain well before using, squeezing the apples with your hands to expel any additional liquid.

ADD THE FILLINGS: Add the apples and rosemary to the bowl. Work the fillings into the dough, about 1 minute.

BULK RISE: Cover the bowl with a damp towel and let rise until double in size. This will take about 8 to 10 hours at room temperature, 70°F (21°C). Alternatively, once fully risen, cover the dough with lightly oiled plastic wrap and chill overnight.

SHAPE AND COAT WITH CHEESE: Line a sheet pan with parchment paper and set aside. Remove the dough onto a lightly floured work surface. Gently pat the dough into a rectangle, pressing out any large air bubbles. Divide into 12 equal pieces, about 85 grams (3 oz) each. Gather the ends, flip the dough over, and roll each piece into a ball. Let rest on the counter while you grab the cheese.

Add the cheese to a wide, shallow bowl or plate. Brush the dough with water, then roll in the cheese to coat the top, bottom, and sides. Transfer the dough to your sheet pan. Repeat with the rest of the dough, placing 3 rolls across and 4 down.

SECOND RISE: Cover the dough and let rest for about 30 to 45 minutes or until noticeably puffy. If working with cold dough, increase the time to 1 hour or more, depending on temperature.

Preheat your oven to 400°F (200°C).

BAKE: Bake the rolls for 25 to 30 minutes or until fully risen and golden brown with blistered, bubbling cheese. They will smell amazing. Cool before serving, although these rolls are delicious warm.

Store at room temperature in a plastic bag for up to 1 day. Reheat before serving for best texture.

GRAB-AND-GO CRANBERRY-PECAN HARVEST BUNS

Makes 12 Buns

If you're looking for a quick, effortless breakfast in the morning, this is it. These buns are hearty and not too sweet, and they have a wonderful chewy texture. Once baked, a drizzle of melted coconut oil will keep the crust tender and soft while adding hints of warm, tropical flavor. The aroma is heavenly. These buns would be perfect for a casual brunch spread, too, served warm with softened butter or whipped cream cheese.

About the Dough: If you'd like to enjoy these buns warm for breakfast, shape the dough directly in the pan and refrigerate overnight. In the morning, just pop them into the oven (don't forget to take the chill off first), and they'll be ready with coffee in no time. You can also toast the pecans for extra flavor. The addition of molasses gives this dough a rich, toffee color and a hint of mild sweetness.

DOUGH
50 g (¼ cup) bubbly, active starter

350 g (1⅓ cups plus 2 tbsp) warm water

40 g (2 tbsp) unsulphured molasses

300 g (2½ cups) all-purpose flour

200 g (1⅔ cups) bread flour

1 g (½ tsp) cinnamon

9 g (1½ tsp) salt

FILLINGS
130 g (1 cup) dried cranberries

65 g (½ cup) chopped pecans

12 g (1 tbsp) sugar

TOPPINGS
20 g (¼ cup) rolled oats

30 g (¼ cup) sunflower seeds

30 g (2 tbsp) coconut oil, melted

A few days before baking, feed your starter until bubbly and active. Store at room temperature until ready to use.

MAKE THE DOUGH: In a large bowl, whisk the starter, water, and molasses together with a fork. Add the flours, cinnamon, and salt. Combine to form a rough dough, then finish mixing by hand to mop up any dry bits of flour. Cover with a damp towel and let rest for 30 minutes. Replenish your starter with fresh flour and water, and store according to preference

While the dough is resting, add the cranberries, pecans, and sugar to a small bowl. Cover with just enough warm water to soak. Drain well before adding to the dough.

ADD THE FILLINGS: Add the fruit and nuts to the bowl. Gently work the fillings into the dough to incorporate, about 1 minute, or until the mass comes together easily.

BULK RISE: Cover the bowl with a damp towel and let rise at room temperature. This will take about 8 to 10 hours at 70°F (21°C).

SHAPE: Line a 9 × 13-inch (23 × 33-cm) baking pan with parchment paper. Set aside.

Remove the dough onto a lightly floured surface. Gently pat the dough into a rectangle, and divide into 12 equal pieces, about 95 grams (3¼ oz) each. Gather the ends, flip the dough over, and shape each piece into a ball. Place into the pan, 3 pieces across and 4 down.

SECOND RISE: Cover the dough with a damp towel and let rest for about 30 minutes to 1 hour, depending on temperature. The buns will begin to touch as they puff up. At this point, you can proceed to the next step or cover the dough in lightly oiled plastic wrap and chill overnight. In the morning, bring to room temperature before baking, about 1 hour.

Preheat your oven to 400°F (200°C). Brush the dough with water and sprinkle with the oats and sunflower seeds, patting down gently to coat.

BAKE: Bake the dough on the center rack for about 40 minutes. Once finished, drizzle some of the coconut oil over the crust while still warm. This will keep the texture soft. Enjoy warm or at room temperature.

These harvest buns will last up to 2 days, stored at room temperature in a plastic bag or airtight container.

EASY PITA POCKETS

Makes 8 Pitas

Sourdough pitas are so light and flavorful, your next desk lunch will make your coworkers envious with excitement. I have to say, these are really fun to make. Not to mention, they're 100% natural and preservative-free. To get your pitas to puff up like hot air balloons, you'll need to preheat your cast iron skillet until piping hot. That's the secret. And guess what else? They bake up in 4 minutes or less.

About the Dough: This dough will feel dry and stiff at first, but after a long rise, it's much easier to work with. You'll also find that between the addition of whole wheat flour and the extended rise, the flavor of these pitas is quite tangy. Shape the dough into little balls before rolling, which makes forming the pita circles a breeze.

100 g (½ cup) bubbly, active starter

180 g (¾ cup) warm water

7 g (1 tsp) honey

15 g (1 tbsp) olive oil

150 g (1¼ cups) all-purpose flour

120 g (1 cup) whole wheat flour

3 g (½ tsp) fine sea salt

A few days before baking, feed your starter until bubbly and active. Store at room temperature until ready to use.

MAKE THE DOUGH: In a medium bowl, whisk the starter, water, honey, and olive oil together with a fork. Add the flours and salt. Mix to combine, then finish by hand until a rough dough forms. Cover with a damp towel and let rest for 30 to 45 minutes. Replenish your starter with fresh flour and water, and store according to preference.

After the dough has rested, work the mass into a semi-smooth ball, about 20 seconds.

BULK RISE: Cover the dough and let rise at room temperature, 70°F (21°C), until double in size, about 6 to 8 hours.

SHAPE: Line a sheet pan with parchment paper and set aside. Remove the dough onto a lightly floured work surface. Divide into 8 pieces, about 65 grams (2¼ oz) each. Pinch the ends, flip the dough over, and roll each piece into a ball. Place onto your sheet pan, seam side down.

SECOND RISE: Cover the dough with a damp towel and let rest until puffy, about 30 minutes to 1 hour. Meanwhile, preheat your oven to 450°F (230°C). Place a cast iron skillet or pizza stone on the bottom rack to heat up.

ROLL THE DOUGH: Generously dust your work surface with flour, then dust the tops of the dough. Working with one ball of dough at a time, roll into a thin circle about ¼ inch (6.3 mm) thick (see tip below). If using a pizza stone, roll out a second ball of dough to bake 2 rounds at a time.

BAKE: Place the dough into your hot skillet and bake for about 3 to 4 minutes. Pitas puff up quickly and cook fast, so keep your eye on them. When finished, transfer to a wire rack; they will deflate slightly as they cool. Finish rolling and baking the rest of the pitas.

These sourdough pitas will stay fresh in a plastic bag for up to 3 to 4 days at room temperature.

TIP: On occasion, pita pockets won't puff up—this happens to the best of us. In addition to using a piping hot skillet, make sure that the dough is evenly rolled, especially around the edges.

OVERNIGHT MINI SOURDOUGH ENGLISH MUFFINS

Makes 10 to 12 Mini English Muffins

Is there anything better than a warm English muffin with melted butter brushed into every nook and cranny? Making them from scratch is easier than you'd think, and you don't even have to turn the oven on—they are cooked in a skillet. These muffins are exceptional toasted, or you can use them for mini breakfast sandwiches. For an authentic touch, split them open with a fork to expose their beautiful craggy holes.

About the Dough: This dough holds up well when chilled, making English muffins perfect for weekend breakfasts. You can make the dough on Friday before you leave the house for the day and refrigerate the whole bowl overnight. Cook fresh on Saturday morning and enjoy. See the tip below for best results.

245 g (1 cup plus 1 tsp) milk, whole or 2%

120 g (½ cup) water

56 g (4 tbsp) unsalted butter, cubed

75 g (heaped ⅓ cup) bubbly, active starter

24 g (2 tbsp) sugar

500 g (4 cups plus 2 tbsp) all-purpose flour

9 g (1½ tsp) salt

Cornmeal or semolina flour, for dusting

A few days before baking, feed your starter until bubbly and active. Store at room temperature until ready to use.

TIP: The trick to cooking English muffins is to find balanced heat. If the flame is too high, the muffins will brown too quickly on the outside, leaving the center undercooked. If this happens, finish baking the muffins in a low-heat oven, about 250°F (130°C), until cooked through. You can also do a test batch first, to gauge your stove-top heat.

MAKE THE DOUGH: In a small saucepan, warm the milk, water, and butter together over low heat or in the microwave. Cool slightly before adding to the dough.

Add the starter and sugar to a large bowl. Slowly pour in the warm milk mixture, while whisking to combine. Add the flour and salt. Mix with a fork to form a rough dough, then finish by hand to fully incorporate the flour. Cover with a damp towel and let rest for 30 minutes. Meanwhile, replenish your starter with fresh flour and water, and store according to preference.

After the dough has rested, work the mass into a semi-smooth ball, about 15 to 20 seconds.

BULK RISE: Cover the bowl with a damp towel and let rise until double in size, about 8 to 10 hours at 70°F (21°C). Once fully risen, cover the dough in lightly oiled plastic wrap and chill it overnight.

SHAPE: In the morning, remove the cold dough onto a floured work surface and let rest for 10 minutes. Line a sheet pan with parchment paper and sprinkle generously with cornmeal to prevent sticking.

With floured hands, pat the dough into a rectangle or oval shape, about ½ inch (1.25 cm) thick. Cut into 10 to 12 rounds using the rim of a drinking glass or mug, about 3 inches (8 cm) in diameter. Place the rounds onto your sheet pan and sprinkle the tops with cornmeal.

SECOND RISE: Cover the dough with a damp towel and let rest until puffy, about 1 hour, depending on temperature.

COOK THE MUFFINS: Warm a large nonstick skillet over low heat. Place a few rounds of dough into the pan to fit comfortably; they do not spread very much when cooking. Cook on one side for about 8 to 10 minutes, checking at the halfway mark for even browning. Adjust the heat if necessary. Flip the muffins over and continue to cook for an additional 8 to 10 minutes. When ready, the muffins should feel lightweight and the sides should spring back when pressed gently.

Transfer the muffins to a wire rack to cool, and cook the remaining rounds of dough in the skillet. When all of the muffins are cooled and ready to serve, split open with a fork along the sides.

These English muffins will stay fresh up to 2 days, stored in a plastic bag at room temperature.

SUNDAY MORNING BAGELS

Makes 8 Bagels

I'm happy to report that homemade bagels are not difficult to make and rival any New York bagel shop. Take my word for it—I'm from New York, the land of pizza and bagels! The dough is quick to put together and the shaping is easy, as the dough is noticeably stiff and can be stretched however you want. I highly recommend eating a warm, chewy, delicious sourdough bagel straight from the oven to experience its one-of-a-kind thin and crispy crust.

About the Dough: Bagels are all about technique, which is a two-step process. First, boil the dough to set the crust, which prevents the dough from rising too much. You can't skip this step, but it's easy—it's just like boiling ravioli. Then bake the bagels for a nice golden crust. For timing, you can break up the process over two days. Make the dough on Saturday evening and allow it to rise overnight. On Sunday morning, shape, boil, and bake.

150 g (¾ cup) bubbly, active starter

250 g (1 cup plus 2 tsp) warm water

24 g (2 tbsp) sugar

500 g (4 cups plus 2 tsp) bread flour

9 g (1½ tsp) fine sea salt

20 g (1 tbsp) honey

Cooking spray or oil, for coating

Mixed seeds, such as poppy, sesame, fennel, flax, and sunflower

A few days before baking, feed your starter until bubbly and active. Store at room temperature until ready to use.

MAKE THE DOUGH: In a large bowl, whisk the starter, water, and sugar together with a fork. Add the flour and salt. Combine to form a rough dough, then finish mixing by hand to fully incorporate the flour. Because this dough is stiff, consider using a stand mixer to give your hands a break; run on low speed for 5 to 6 minutes to combine. Cover the dough with a damp towel and let rest for 45 minutes to 1 hour. Meanwhile, replenish your starter with fresh flour and water. Store according to preference.

After the dough has rested, work the mass into a semi-smooth ball, about 15 to 20 seconds.

BULK RISE: Cover the bowl with a damp towel and let rise until double in size, about 8 to 10 hours at room temperature, 70°F (21°C).

SHAPE: Line a sheet pan with a nonstick silicone mat or parchment paper. If using parchment, lightly coat with cooking spray or oil to prevent sticking.

Remove the dough onto a non-floured work surface. Flatten the dough into a rectangle and divide into 8 equal pieces, about 115 grams (4 oz) each. Gather the ends, flip the dough over, and roll each piece into a ball. Let the dough rest on your sheet pan for 10 to 15 minutes to relax the gluten.

Working with one ball of dough at a time, poke a hole straight through the center. Lift up the dough, insert both index fingers through the center hole, and barrel roll to gently stretch the opening to about the size of a walnut. When finished, place the dough back onto your sheet pan. It's okay if the hole shrinks slightly. Repeat shaping the remaining dough.

SECOND RISE: Cover the dough with a damp towel and let rest for 15 to 20 minutes. The dough will puff up only slightly at this stage.

Meanwhile, bring a medium pot of water to a boil. Add the honey and whisk well to dissolve. Preheat your oven to 425°F (220°C). Add the seeds to a rimmed tray or shallow bowl.

BOIL THE BAGELS: Add 2 to 3 bagels into the pot and wait for them to float to the top, about 10 seconds, or they will float right away. Simmer for 30 seconds on each side for a thin crust. Using a slotted spoon, transfer the bagels back the sheet pan you used earlier, placing them rounded side up. Once slightly cool but still wet, dip the rounded side of the bagels into the seeds to coat. Place back onto the sheet pan and finish boiling the rest of the bagels.

(continued)

SUNDAY MORNING BAGELS (CONT.)

BAKE: Bake the bagels for about 20 to 25 minutes. Flip them over to briefly cook the bottom side, about 1 to 2 minutes or less. When ready, your bagels will be puffed up and light golden brown, and they will feel light to the touch. Transfer to a wire rack to cool, but indulge yourself and eat one (or two) warm.

The chewy texture of bagels is best enjoyed when made fresh. Store in a plastic bag at room temperature for up to 2 days. Bagels also freeze well; freeze them whole or sliced, covered in plastic wrap and a layer of foil, for up to 3 months.

TIP: Sometimes your bagels will have a smooth surface, and other times they might feel bumpy or have small blisters. This all depends on how the dough was fermented, the temperature, and overall handling. Don't worry about this too much, as the appearance has no bearing on flavor.

VARIATION: For cinnamon raisin bagels, add 6 grams (2 tsp) of cinnamon, or 3 grams (1 tsp) pumpkin pie spice plus 3 grams (1 tsp) of cinnamon, to the dry ingredients. While the dough is resting, soak 80 grams (½ cup) of raisins in warm water. Drain well before kneading them into the dough to incorporate.

OVERNIGHT SOURDOUGH BIALYS WITH CARAMELIZED ONIONS and GOAT CHEESE

Makes 12 Small Bialys

In any New York deli, right next the bagels, you'll find the bialys. Bialys are similar to bagels, but they are lighter in texture, boast a more tender crumb, and are baked straight through, not boiled. They are very similar to rolls. You'll also find a small dip in the center which can be filled with a variety of toppings, including onions, which is the most traditional. Or, omit the goat cheese and serve toasted with cream cheese and the toppings of your choice.

About the Dough: This dough rises conveniently overnight to shape and bake in the morning. To make the most of your time, you can prepare the onion mixture up to 2 days in advance.

DOUGH

50 g (¼ cup) bubbly, active starter

375 g (1½ cups plus 1 tbsp) cool water

500 g (4 cups plus 2 tbsp) all-purpose flour

9 g (1½ tsp) fine sea salt

FILLING

15 g (1 tbsp) olive oil

14 g (1 tbsp) unsalted butter

1 large red or yellow onion, chopped into small pieces

3 thyme sprigs, leaves picked, plus extra to serve

Salt and freshly ground black pepper

4 oz (114 g) goat cheese, crumbled

Mixed seeds, such as poppy, sesame, fennel, flax, and sunflower

A few days before baking, feed your starter until bubbly and active. Store at room temperature until ready to use.

MAKE THE DOUGH: In the evening, whisk the starter and water together in a large bowl. Add the flour and salt. Mix to combine, then incorporate by hand until a rough dough forms. Cover the bowl with a damp towel and let rest for 30 minutes to 1 hour, depending on your schedule. Replenish your starter with fresh flour and water, and store according to preference.

After the dough has rested, work the mass into a semi-smooth ball, about 15 seconds.

BULK RISE: Cover the bowl with a damp towel and let rise overnight at room temperature, 70°F (21°C), about 12 to 18 hours. The dough will double or triple in size when ready, with a few bubbles on the surface.

DIVIDE: In the morning, line a sheet pan with parchment paper. Sprinkle heavily with flour to prevent sticking. Set aside. Remove the dough onto a lightly floured work surface. Divide into 12 pieces, about 75 grams (2½ oz) each. Gather the ends, flip the dough over, and roll each piece into a ball. Place the dough onto your lined sheet pan, 3 pieces across and 4 down.

SECOND RISE: Cover the dough with a damp towel and let rest for 1 to 1½ hours, or until puffy.

PREPARE THE FILLING: Meanwhile, in a large skillet, warm the olive oil and butter over low heat. Add the chopped onions and thyme, and season lightly with salt and pepper. Sauté until soft and translucent, but not yet caramelized, about 7 to 10 minutes. Remove the pan from the heat to cool before topping the dough.

Preheat your oven to 450°F (230°C).

SHAPE AND ASSEMBLE: Lightly dust the tops of the dough with flour. Working with one piece of dough at a time, use three fingers to make an impression into the center. Then, using your fingertips, gently push and stretch the center indentation to about 2 to 3 inches (5 to 8 cm). If the dough starts to resist, let rest for 10 minutes and try again. Repeat this technique until you have finished with all of the dough.

Lightly brush the outside of the dough with water. Spoon some of the cooled onions into the center and top with goat cheese. Sprinkle the outside of the dough with seeds.

BAKE: Bake the bialys on the center rack for 10 to 12 minutes. They will puff up and turn light golden in color, and the onions will become caramelized. Transfer to a wire rack to cool before serving.

Bialys are best enjoyed on the same day. Store at room temperature in a plastic bag, up to 1 day.

ROASTED GARLIC SOURDOUGH KNOTS
with PECORINO

Makes 10 Knots

I was never a huge fan of garlic knots. The amount of raw garlic would not only annihilate my taste buds, but anyone in my path would be blasted with garlic-scented dragon breath. But then there's *roasted* garlic. Sweet roasted garlic cloves, caramelized to perfection, are folded into this sourdough with fresh thyme for a light and tasty twist.

About the Dough: A blend of all-purpose and bread flour makes the dough light yet gives it enough structure to create that essential chewy texture. Once fully risen, the dough is chilled overnight to deepen the flavor and make shaping easier to handle. The garlic can also be roasted ahead of time and stored in the freezer until ready to use.

ROASTED GARLIC

1 head of fresh garlic

15 g (1 tbsp) olive oil, plus more for brushing

DOUGH

50 g (¼ cup) bubbly, active starter

240 g (1 cup) warm water

120 g (1 cup) all-purpose flour

180 g (1½ cups) bread flour

5 g (1 tsp) fine sea salt

6 thyme sprigs, leaves picked

HERB AND CHEESE TOPPING

28 g (2 tbsp) unsalted butter

7 g (2 tbsp) chopped parsley

Pecorino cheese, to taste

A few days before baking, feed your starter until bubbly and active. Store at room temperature until ready to use.

ROAST THE GARLIC: In the morning, preheat your oven to 400°F (200°C). Lay the garlic on its side and slice off the top third to reveal the inside cloves. Wrap the garlic in foil and drizzle with olive oil to coat. Roast on a sheet pan for 45 minutes to 1 hour. The garlic should be soft and caramelized when ready.

MAKE THE DOUGH: In a medium bowl, whisk the starter and water together with a fork. Add the flours, salt, and thyme leaves. Mix to form a shaggy dough, mopping up all the dry bits of flour on the side of the bowl. Cover with a damp towel and let rest until the garlic has finished roasting. Replenish your starter with fresh flour and water, and store according to preference.

ADD THE GARLIC: When the garlic is cool enough to handle, squeeze the cloves directly into the bowl. Gently knead to incorporate, about 20 seconds, pressing the garlic into the dough.

BULK RISE: Cover the bowl with a damp towel and let rise at room temperature until double in size. This will take about 8 to 10 hours at 70°F (21°C). Once fully risen, cover the dough in lightly oiled plastic wrap and chill overnight.

SHAPE: When ready to bake, line a sheet pan with parchment paper. Remove the cold dough onto a well-floured surface and let rest for 10 minutes. Divide the dough into 10 strips, about 60 grams (2 oz) each. Grab the ends of each strip and stretch gently to tie a knot. It's just like tying your shoe laces, minus the bow. Place onto your sheet pan and shape the rest of the dough. When finished, lightly brush the knots with olive oil.

SECOND RISE: Cover the dough and let rest until noticeably puffy, about 1 hour or more, depending on temperature.

Preheat your oven to 400°F (200°C).

BAKE: Bake the knots on the center rack for 20 to 25 minutes, or until light golden brown. Meanwhile, melt the butter in a small saucepan or in the microwave. Chop the parsley and grab the cheese.

When the knots have finished baking, add them to a large bowl. Drizzle some of the melted butter over the top and sprinkle with the parsley and cheese. Toss well to coat. Arrange the warm knots on a serving platter or devour straight from the bowl.

Garlic knots are best enjoyed on the same day they are made.

CRISPY SOURDOUGH GRISSINI

Makes About 24 Grissini

These crispy Italian breadsticks are hand-pulled, not rolled, which makes each one rustic and unique. They are delicious plain or dressed up, as I've done here with paper-thin slices of prosciutto, creamy blue cheese, pears, and dates for a tantalizing appetizer spread. The next time you're hosting a dinner party, imagine a few platters or jars of homemade grissini lining your table as an edible center piece.

About the Dough: For this method, the bulk dough is chilled overnight once fully risen. The firm, cold dough gives you a bit more control when pulling and twisting it.

DOUGH

75 g (heaped ⅓ cup) bubbly, active starter

150 g (½ cup plus 2 tbsp) warm water

12 g (1 tbsp) sugar

240 g (2 cups) all-purpose flour

5 g (1 tsp) fine sea salt

Oil, for coating

Cornmeal or semolina flour, for dusting

SERVING OPTIONS

Prosciutto slices

Blue cheese wedges

Soft dates

Sliced pears

Honeycomb

A few days before baking, feed your starter until bubbly and active. Store at room temperature until ready to use.

MAKE THE DOUGH: In the morning, whisk the starter, water, and sugar together in a medium bowl. Add the flour and salt. Combine to form a rough dough with no lumps of flour remaining. Cover with a damp towel and let rest for 30 minutes. Replenish your starter with fresh flour and water, and store according to preference.

BULK RISE: Cover the bowl with a damp towel and let rise until double in size, about 8 to 10 hours at room temperature, 70°F (21°C). Once fully risen, cover the dough loosely in oiled plastic wrap and chill overnight.

DIVIDE AND SHAPE: Preheat your oven to 425°F (220°C). Line 2 sheet pans with nonstick silicone mats or parchment paper. Dust heavily with cornmeal to prevent sticking.

Remove the dough onto a lightly oiled work surface. Divide it into 2 equal portions and let rest for 10 minutes. Working with one portion at a time, roll the dough into a long oval shape, about 12 × 5 inches (30 × 13 cm) with a floured rolling pin. Keeping the width narrow is important, as the dough will stretch in length as you hand-pull the grissini. Let rest for 10 minutes before shaping.

With a lightly oiled pizza wheel or bench scraper, cut the dough across into ½-inch (1.3-cm) strips. You should end up with about 12 strips in total. To shape, grab the ends of the dough and lift it up while gently twisting to fit the short end of your sheet pan. If there is any resistance, let the dough rest for 5 to 10 minutes and try again. You'll notice that the weight of the dough will do most of the stretching for you.

SECOND RISE: Cover the dough with a damp towel and let rest for 10 minutes. Meanwhile, roll, cut, and shape the remaining portion of dough.

BAKE: Bake one sheet pan of dough for about 12 to 15 minutes, or until light golden. Then bake the second sheet pan of dough. Cool completely before serving to ensure extra crispiness.

Grissini will last 2 to 3 days when stored at room temperature in an air-tight container.

VARIATION: After the dough has rested, finely chop 40 grams (⅓ cup) kalamata olives and knead them into the dough. Add a sprinkle of flour to adjust the texture if it seems too sticky. Proceed with the rest of the recipe as indicated above.

SOFT SEMOLINA BREADSTICKS
with BUTTERY CRUMBS

Makes 14 Soft Breadsticks

Incredibly soft, with a lovely chewy texture, these breadsticks will make a wonderful addition to your sourdough arsenal. Once baked, the breadsticks are pressed into a mixture of seasoned bread crumbs and Parmesan cheese for a delicious, crunchy topping. Dunk into warm tomato sauce or my Zesty Garlic and Herb Oil (page 183). My kids go crazy over these.

About the Dough: If you've made the Crispy Sourdough Grissini on page 125, the gentle hand-pulled shaping method for these breadsticks is very similar. However, when making soft breadsticks, make sure you don't stretch the dough too long or they will bake up thin and crunchy instead.

BREADSTICKS

50 g (¼ cup) bubbly, active starter

350 g (1⅓ cups plus 2 tbsp) warm water

12 g (1 tbsp) sugar

80 g (½ cup) semolina flour, plus more for dusting

420 g (3½ cups) bread flour

9 g (1½ tsp) fine sea salt

Olive oil, for coating

TOPPING

30 g (¼ cup) Italian seasoned breadcrumbs

40 g (¼ cup) ground Parmesan cheese

42 g (3 tbsp) unsalted butter

A few days before baking, feed your starter until bubbly and active. Store at room temperature until ready to use.

MAKE THE DOUGH: In a large bowl, whisk the starter, water, and sugar together with a fork. Add the flours and salt. Combine to form a rough dough, then finish by hand to fully incorporate the flour. Cover with a damp towel and let rest for 30 minutes. Replenish your starter with fresh flour and water, and store according to preference.

After the dough has rested, work the mass into a semi-smooth ball, about 15 seconds.

BULK RISE: Cover the dough with a damp towel and let rise at room temperature until double in size, about 8 to 10 hours at 70°F (21°C).

SHAPE: Line 2 sheet pans with parchment paper and dust with semolina flour.

Lightly brush your work surface with oil. Remove the dough onto the surface and let rest for 10 minutes. Then gently flatten the dough into a long rectangle, about 14 × 5 inches (36 × 13 cm). Cut across into fourteen 1-inch (2.5-cm) thick strips. Divide evenly between both sheet pans. The breadsticks will naturally stretch in length as you transfer the dough.

SECOND RISE: Cover the dough and let rest until puffy, about 30 minutes depending on temperature.

CRUMB TOPPING: Meanwhile, toast the bread crumbs in a small nonstick pan, stirring often, until golden, about 3 to 5 minutes. When finished, transfer the breadcrumbs to a plate to cool. Add the Parmesan cheese and mix to combine. Wipe out the pan and melt the butter over low heat. Set aside.

Preheat your oven to 425°F (220°C). Lightly brush the dough with some of the melted butter, reserving what's left in the pan to adhere the crumb topping to the baked breadsticks.

BAKE: Place both sheet pans into the oven and bake for about 13 to 15 minutes. Swap racks halfway through baking for even coloring. You can also bake one sheet pan at a time, if you prefer. When ready, the breadsticks will be pale golden in color and feel noticeably lightweight.

To serve, brush the breadsticks with the reserved melted butter. Press into the breadcrumb topping to coat. Enjoy warm or at room temperature, with extra napkins.

These breadsticks are best enjoyed fresh. They can be frozen, without the crumb topping, once completely cool. Layer them between sheets of parchment and cover in plastic wrap and foil. Freeze up to 3 months.

CIABATTA

Makes 2 to 3 Loaves

Ciabatta, or "slipper" in Italian, is a wonderful rustic bread known for its light and airy holes. It's perfect for dunking and makes the best panini sandwiches. The secret to ciabatta lies within both the recipe and method, so for best results, make sure to implement the techniques below. It's well worth it, because this sourdough slipper will be unlike any you've ever tried.

About the Dough: Ciabatta is a very wet, sticky dough, probably the wettest dough in this book. Using a stand mixer simplifies the preparation and adds a wonderful lightness to the finished loaf. Stretch and folds are important for strength, and help to open up the crumb. Heads up: Ciabatta dough will appear lifeless after it has been shaped, but don't fret. It will bounce back once baked.

100 g (½ cup) bubbly, active starter

400 g (1⅔ cups) warm water, plus 240 g (1 cup) water for the oven

250 g (2 cups plus 1 tbsp) bread flour

250 g (2 cups plus 1 tbsp) all-purpose flour

9 g (1½ tsp) fine sea salt

Oil, for coating

A few days before baking, feed your starter until bubbly and active. Store at room temperature until ready to use.

MAKE THE DOUGH: Add the starter, water, flours, and salt to the bowl of a stand mixer fitted with the paddle attachment. Mix on low speed to combine. The dough will look shaggy and sticky; scrape down the sides of the bowl as needed. When finished, cover with a damp towel and let rest for 1 hour. Meanwhile, replenish your starter with fresh flour and water, and store according to preference.

After the dough has rested, switch to the dough hook and knead on medium speed for 10 to 13 minutes. The dough will continue to look wet and sticky, but after kneading, it will become shiny and smooth, like taffy. Transfer the dough into a new bowl lightly coated in oil. Cover with a damp towel and let rest for 30 minutes.

BULK RISE WITH STRETCH AND FOLDS: With lightly wet hands, grab a portion of the dough, stretch it upward, and fold it over toward the center of the bowl. Give the bowl a one-quarter turn and repeat until you have come full circle to complete your first set. Repeat this technique, about 3 to 4 sets, spaced 15 to 30 minutes apart (see page 194).

When your stretch and folds are complete, cover the dough and let rise at room temperature until double or triple in size. This will take about 7 to 10 hours at 70°F (21°C).

DIVIDE AND SHAPE: Line a sheet pan with parchment paper and dust heavily with flour. Set aside.

Gently coax the dough onto well-floured work surface. Ciabatta dough will stick to everything in sight, so feel free to use extra flour as needed. With floured hands, gently fold the dough in half to create a rectangle, taking care not to deflate the air bubbles. Let rest for 10 minutes. Divide the dough into 2 or 3 pieces with a bench scraper dipped in water to prevent sticking. Transfer each piece to your sheet pan. Dimple the dough just a few times with your fingertips.

SECOND RISE: Cover the dough and let rest for 1 hour. The dough won't puff very much at this stage, but don't worry—this is characteristic of ciabatta.

Preheat your oven to 500°F (260°C). Place a 9 × 13-inch (23 × 33-cm) pan on the bottom rack to heat up.

BAKE: With floured hands, coax your fingertips underneath the dough and flip it over so that the dimpled side faces down. This helps to redistribute the air bubbles during baking. Pour 240 grams (1 cup) of water into the hot pan to create steam. Place the ciabatta on the center rack, and then reduce the heat to 425°F (220°C). Bake for about 25 to 30 minutes, or until the loaves are golden brown. Remove to a wire rack and cool for 1 hour before slicing.

Ciabatta is best enjoyed on the same day it's made. Once completely cool, store the loaves in a plastic bag at room temperature, up to 1 day.

OVERNIGHT BAGUETTE TWISTS

Makes 3 Small Baguettes

In culinary school, having access to homemade baguettes completely ruined me, or rather, set a high bar for what the ultimate French bread should taste like. Nothing compares to the thin, crackly crust of a good baguette! However, baguettes can be tricky to make and take a bit of practice. For this recipe, I've skipped the traditional shaping, resting, and scoring method to make them more approachable for every day. In my humble opinion, they're just as delicious.

About the Dough: For extra flavor, white whole wheat flour is added for a hint of mild sweetness. After the dough is shaped, it does not need a long second rise; 10 to 15 minutes is sufficient. Fresh thyme is pressed into the dough for a subtle, earthy flavor.

50 g (¼ cup) bubbly, active starter
360 g (1½ cups plus 1 tsp) cool water
400 g (3⅓ cups) all-purpose flour
40 g (⅓ cup) white whole wheat flour
9 g (1½ tsp) fine sea salt
6 thyme sprigs, leaves picked

A few days before baking, feed your starter until bubbly and active. Store at room temperature until ready to use.

MAKE THE DOUGH: In the evening, whisk the starter and water together in a large bowl with a fork. Add the flours and salt. Mix to combine, then finish by hand to form a rough dough. Cover the bowl with a damp towel and let rest for 30 minutes. Replenish your starter with fresh flour and water, and store according to preference.

After the dough has rested, gently work the mass into a semi-smooth ball, about 1 minute.

BULK RISE: Cover the bowl with a damp towel and let the dough rise overnight. This will take about 12 to 18 hours at room temperature, 70°F (21°C). The dough will double or triple in size when ready.

DIVIDE: In the morning, remove the dough onto a heavily floured work surface. With floured hands, fold the dough in half like a book. Cover and let rest for 10 to 15 minutes or more, until the dough is relaxed enough to shape. Meanwhile, line a sheet pan with parchment paper and dust with flour. Preheat your oven to 450°F (230°C).

Sprinkle the dough with flour. Cut the dough horizontally into 3 equal portions using a bench scraper dipped in water to prevent sticking. Working in batches, gently roll the dough over, about 1 to 2 times to coat in the excess flour.

SHAPE: To shape, lift up the dough and stretch gently to fit the long end of your sheet pan. Then twist the dough into a log, starting at the top and working your way to the bottom. The shape does not need to resemble a perfect corkscrew—a rustic-style design is what you're aiming for. Sprinkle some of the thyme leaves over the dough, pressing gently to adhere. Repeat with the remaining portions of dough.

SECOND RISE: Cover the dough with a damp towel and let rest for 10 to 15 minutes. The dough will not puff up very much during this stage.

BAKE: Place the sheet pan into the oven and reduce the heat to 425°F (220°C). Bake the baguettes for 30 to 35 minutes, until deep golden brown. Transfer to a wire rack and cool for 30 minutes before slicing.

Baguettes are best consumed fresh, as they tend to go stale quickly. Serve warm or share with the neighbors.

BREAD ART

Once you get the hang of making bread, it's fun to create different shapes and designs. To streamline the process, you'll work with just a few doughs so your artistic side can take center stage. Then you'll get to indulge in many sourdough creations, including my creamy Make-Ahead Spinach and Artichoke Dip Braid (page 144) or Salted Chocolate Caramel Knot (page 143). And remember, you can always practice your shaping techniques with a few pieces of playdough before attempting the real thing. I do it all the time.

BAKED CAMEMBERT WREATH

Makes 1 Wreath

Is there anything more welcoming than a beautiful, edible wreath? The French call this particular design "Pain D'Epi" as its whimsical shape bears resemblance to golden wheat stalks. A wheel of soft Camembert cheese studded with garlic and rosemary is placed into the center; it gets all creamy and delicious when baked. This sourdough is perfect for entertaining and sharing with friends.

About the Dough: To really enjoy the combination of warm, melted cheese and crusty bread for dunking, this wreath is best baked right before serving. For timing, you can make the dough in the morning and chill the whole bowl overnight once fully risen. You will need good kitchen shears or sharp scissors to snip the dough.

WREATH DOUGH

75 g (heaped ⅓ cup) bubbly, active starter

285 g (1 cup plus 3 tbsp) warm water

480 g (4 cups) bread flour, plus more for dusting

9 g (1½ tsp) fine sea salt

FILLING

1 small wheel of Camembert cheese

1 clove of garlic, sliced paper-thin

1 sprig of fresh rosemary, leaves picked

Olive oil, for drizzling

A few days before baking, feed your starter until bubbly and active. Store at room temperature until ready to use.

MAKE THE DOUGH: In a large bowl, whisk the starter and water together with a fork. Add the flour and salt. Combine to form a rough dough, then finish mixing by hand to incorporate. Cover with a damp towel and let rest for 30 minutes. Replenish your starter with fresh flour and water, and store according to preference.

After the dough has rested, gently work the mass into a semi-smooth ball, about 15 seconds.

BULK RISE: Cover the dough with a damp towel and let rise at room temperature until double in size, about 8 to 10 hours at 70°F (21°C). Once fully risen, cover the dough in lightly oiled plastic wrap and chill it overnight, if desired.

SHAPE: Remove the dough onto a lightly floured work surface. Shape the dough into a round and let rest for 10 minutes. Meanwhile, line a sheet pan with parchment paper.

Generously dust the surface of the dough with flour, and rub evenly to coat. Poke a hole in the center, going straight through the bottom. Using both hands, stretch the hole to about 5 to 6 inches (13 to 15 cm) or to the approximate size of the wheel of Camembert cheese. Then place the dough onto your sheet pan.

Remove the cheese and wax paper from its carton and set aside. Place the empty carton into the center of the dough, stretching the sides to fit snugly.

SECOND RISE: Cover the dough and let rest until slightly puffy, about 15 to 30 minutes. If using chilled dough, allow for more time at this stage. Preheat your oven to 450°F (230°C).

PREPARE THE CHEESE: While the dough is resting, turn the cheese onto its side and slice off the white rind to expose the creamy inside. Top with the sliced garlic. Tuck some of the rosemary into the cheese and drizzle lightly with olive oil to coat. Chill until the dough has finished resting.

CUT THE DOUGH: Using kitchen shears dipped in flour, make your first V-shaped cut into the dough. Do this by holding the shears on a 45° angle (not straight up and down), and making the cut about 1½ inches (4 cm) deep. The cut will look like a small leaf. Continue to cut the dough, fanning it out as you go around the wreath. When finished, place the chilled cheese into the carton in the middle of the wreath.

BAKE: Bake the dough on the center rack for 25 to 30 minutes. The dough will turn a lovely golden brown with specks of flour around the edges. The cheese will be creamy, melted and bubbly. Cool on the sheet pan for 30 to 45 minutes before serving.

This sourdough wreath is best enjoyed warm on the day it's made.

ALMOST NO-KNEAD FOUGASSE

Makes 1 Large Fougasse

Traditionally, fougasse can be found stacked throughout the bakeries in the south of France, topped with all kinds of dried herbs, spices, and even cheese. Now you can experience this taste right in your very own kitchen with very little effort and planning at all. It's fun and simple to do, and it's a creative way to show off your shaping skills. Try presenting this sourdough version at your next gathering for a delicious bread to enchant your guests.

About the Dough: Fougasse is best eaten warm, straight from the oven. For timing, you can rise the dough overnight, shape it the next day, and then chill until ready to score and bake, which is what I do when planning to serve this for guests. You'll also need a small, sharp knife or razor blade for cutting the leaf-shaped design into the dough.

DOUGH

50 g (¼ cup) bubbly, active starter

270 g (1 cup plus 2 tbsp) warm water

330 g (2¾ cups) bread flour

15 g (2 tbsp) whole wheat flour

5 g (1 tsp) fine sea salt

Cornmeal or semolina, for coating the pan

TOPPINGS

Olive oil, for brushing

2 g (2 tsp) Herbes de Provence

Parmesan cheese, to taste

A few days before baking, feed your starter until bubbly and active. Store at room temperature until ready to use.

MAKE THE DOUGH: Whisk the starter and water in a medium bowl with a fork. Add the flours and salt. Mix to combine, then finish by hand until a rough dough forms. Cover the bowl with a damp towel and let rest for 30 minutes. Replenish your starter with fresh flour and water, and store according to preference.

After the dough has rested, gently work the mass into a fairly smooth ball, about 15 seconds.

BULK RISE: Cover the bowl with a damp towel and let rise at room temperature until the dough has doubled in size. This will take about 8 to 10 hours, at 70°F (21°C).

SHAPE: Line a sheet pan with parchment paper or a nonstick silicone mat. Sprinkle generously with cornmeal to prevent sticking. Remove the dough onto the sheet pan and let rest for 10 minutes. Gently flatten the dough into a 10-inch (25-cm) rectangle or oval shape, about ½ inch (1.25 cm) thick. Don't worry about being precise with your shaping—the dough should look rustic, not perfect.

SECOND RISE: Cover the dough and let rest at room temperature until it is noticeably puffy, about 1 hour. *Note:* If you are planning to bake later in the day or evening, cover the dough with lightly oiled plastic wrap and transfer the sheet pan to the fridge. Return to room temperature before scoring and baking, about 1 hour.

Preheat your oven to 450°F (230°C).

SCORE: To create a leaf shape design, make a long cut down the center of the dough, leaving a small border at the top and bottom. Then make 3 smaller cuts on each side. With lightly oiled fingertips, gently stretch each cut open, to about 1½ inches (4 cm).

Brush the surface of the dough with olive oil. Sprinkle evenly with the Herbes de Provence.

BAKE: Bake on the center rack for about 25 to 30 minutes, or until light golden brown. Remove from the oven, and cool for 10 minutes. Then lightly brush with olive oil. Sprinkle generously with the Parmesan cheese to taste, patting it down gently as you go. Serve warm, family-style, for everyone to tear and share.

This fougasse is best enjoyed on the day it's made. The thin crust-to-crumb ratio has a tendency to go stale quickly.

RASPBERRY GINGERSNAP TWIST

Makes 1 Twist

This scrumptious sourdough twist is what you'll crave in the late afternoon with a hot cup of coffee or tea. Raspberries and chocolate are swirled into the dough with a surprise secret ingredient: gingersnap cookies. Crushed and sprinkled over the filling, the gingersnaps not only add flavor and crunch but also act as a binding element that makes the dough easier to work with when shaping. Plus, raspberry and ginger get along famously. You'll love the combination.

About the Dough: This sweet dough is so versatile, it can be used to create many types of shapes and designs. It's supple and smooth and doesn't stick easily when rolled, especially when you lightly oil your work surface. Follow the step-by-step photos to get a better idea of the shaping technique.

SWEET DOUGH

160 g (⅔ cup) milk, whole or 2%

42 g (3 tbsp) unsalted butter, divided

1 large egg

100 g (½ cup) bubbly, active starter

24 g (2 tbsp) sugar

300 g (2½ cups) all-purpose flour

3 g (½ tsp) fine sea salt

Oil, for coating

FILLING

40 g (2 tbsp) raspberry jam

20 g (¼ cup) crushed gingersnap cookies

1 g (½ tsp) cinnamon

Small handful of chocolate chips, chopped, or mini chocolate chips

Powdered sugar, for dusting

Handful of raspberries

A few days before baking, feed your starter until bubbly and active. Store at room temperature until ready to use.

MAKE THE DOUGH: Warm the milk and 28 grams (2 tbsp) of butter in a small saucepan or in the microwave. Cool slightly before using.

Add the egg, starter, and sugar to the bowl of a stand mixer. Mix to combine using the paddle attachment. With the machine running, slowly pour in the warm milk mixture. Add the flour and salt, and continue mixing until a rough dough forms, about 1 minute. Scrape down the sides of the bowl as needed. Cover with a damp towel and let rest for 30 minutes.

Meanwhile, replenish your starter with fresh flour and water, and store according to preference.

After the dough has rested, switch to the dough hook and knead on medium-low speed, about 6 to 8 minutes. The dough should be soft and pull away from the sides of the bowl when ready. If the dough seems sticky at this point, add a sprinkle of flour to adjust the consistency.

BULK RISE: Transfer the dough to a new, lightly oiled bowl. Cover with a damp towel and let rise at room temperature until double in size, about 8 to 10 hours at 70°F (21°C).

ASSEMBLE AND SHAPE: Line a sheet pan with parchment paper or a nonstick silicone mat. Set aside.

Remove the dough onto a lightly oiled work surface to prevent sticking. Let rest for 5 to 10 minutes, to make it easier to roll. With a floured rolling pin, roll the dough into a large rectangle, about 15 × 10 inches (38 × 25 cm). Spread the raspberry jam over the dough using a small rubber spatula or the back of a spoon, leaving ½-inch (1.25-cm) border around the edges. Sprinkle the crushed gingersnap cookies, cinnamon, and chocolate chips over the jam.

Working with the short end of the dough, roll it into a tight log, ending up with the seam side down. Lift both ends and transfer to your lined sheet pan. The dough will stretch slightly. Cover the dough with a damp towel and chill until slightly firm, about 30 minutes to 1 hour or more.

Using a large serrated knife, halve the dough lengthwise to reveal the inside layers, keeping ½ inch (1.25 cm) intact at the bottom. Starting at the bottom, crisscross the two halves with the layered sections facing up. Continue to overlap the dough until you have created a complete twist. Gently pinch and tuck the ends under to seal.

Melt the remaining 14 grams (1 tbsp) of butter in a small saucepan or in the microwave.

(continued)

RASPBERRY GINGERSNAP TWIST (CONT.)

SECOND RISE: Brush the surface and sides of the dough with the melted butter. Cover and let rest until noticeably puffy, about 1 hour, depending on temperature.

Preheat your oven to 400°F (200°C).

BAKE: Bake the dough on the center rack for about 20 to 25 minutes. Reduce the heat to 350°F (180°C) and bake for an additional 10 to 15 minutes. The twist will puff up beautifully and turn light golden brown when ready. Some of the filling will bubble and caramelize along the sides.

Once completely cool, dust with powdered sugar and top with fresh raspberries. Cut into slices and enjoy.

This bread is best eaten on the day it's made. Cover in plastic wrap and store at room temperature for up to 2 days.

SALTED CHOCOLATE CARAMEL KNOT

Makes 1 Knot

Waiting for this sourdough to cool will be the longest, most agonizing 30 minutes of your life. Just try to resist a warm slice filled with chocolate hazelnut spread and rich, dulce de leche caramel! I use Maldon sea salt flakes to sprinkle over the filling, which creates the perfect balance of salty-sweet flavor. Just a heads-up: This salt is different from the fine sea salt used for bread doughs. They look like small snowflake crystals.

About the Dough: The secret to using this technique without getting chocolate and caramel all over your hands (although I can think of worse things) is to refrigerate the dough after you roll it. Once it's firmer, it will be easier to cut, and the beautiful layers will stay intact.

DOUGH

1 recipe Sweet Dough (page 138)

Oil, for coating

FILLING

120 g (½ cup) chocolate hazelnut spread, such as Nutella

60 g (2 tbsp) dulce de leche, plus more as needed

Flaky sea salt

Powdered sugar, for decoration

A few days before baking, feed your starter until bubbly and active. Store at room temperature until ready to use.

MAKE THE DOUGH: Make the recipe for Sweet Dough following the method for the Raspberry Gingersnap Twist (page 138). After the bulk rise is complete, proceed to the next step.

ASSEMBLE AND SHAPE: Line a sheet pan with parchment paper and dust with flour. You can also use a nonstick silicone mat.

Remove the dough onto a lightly oiled work surface to prevent sticking. Rest the dough for 5 to 10 minutes before rolling. With a floured rolling pin, roll the dough into a large rectangle, about 18 × 12 inches (46 × 30 cm). Spread the Nutella over the dough, leaving ½-inch (1.25-cm) border around the edges. Spoon some of the dulce de leche over the chocolate and lightly sprinkle with the flaky sea salt.

Starting with the long end, roll the dough into a tight log, ending with the seam side down. Trim the ends of the dough and transfer to your sheet pan. Cover the dough with a damp towel and chill until slightly firm, about 30 minutes to 1 hour or more. Meanwhile, line the bottom and sides of a 10-inch (25-cm) springform pan with parchment paper.

When the dough is ready, halve it lengthwise, keeping ½ inch (1.25 cm) intact at the bottom. It's best to use a large serrated knife for this. Starting at the bottom, overlap both halves, keeping the layered sections facing up. Continue to overlap the dough until you have made a full twist. Then form the dough into a knot, gently tucking it under and pinching the ends to seal. Place the dough into the springform pan.

SECOND RISE: Cover the dough and let rest until puffy, about 1 hour, depending on temperature.

Preheat your oven to 400°F (200°C).

BAKE: Place the dough onto the center rack and bake for about 20 minutes. Reduce the heat to 350°F (180°C) and bake for an additional 10 to 15 minutes. Remove from the oven, and cool for 30 minutes before dusting with powdered sugar to serve.

This sourdough knot will stay fresh up to 1 day, covered in plastic wrap and stored at room temperature.

MAKE-AHEAD STUFFED SPINACH *and* ARTICHOKE DIP BRAID

Makes 1 Large Braid

Fan of spinach and artichoke dip? Imagine all of that rich and creamy goodness stuffed inside sourdough bread, with plenty of mozzarella and parmesan cheese to wow your taste buds. This is a bread to impress. Plus, both the filling and dough can be made ahead of time, to suit your schedule.

About the Dough: This recipe uses the same dough as the Baked Camembert Wreath (page 134). It's a nice, strong dough, perfect for rolling and shaping. A pizza wheel is handy for cutting the dough into strips, if you have one.

DOUGH
1 recipe Wreath dough (page 134)

FILLING
15 g (1 tbsp) olive oil

1 red or yellow onion, diced

110 g (1 cup) marinated artichoke hearts, drained and chopped

1 clove of garlic, minced

230 g (8 oz) baby spinach

Salt and freshly ground black pepper, to taste

30 g (2 tbsp) sour cream or Greek yogurt

50 g (¼ cup) cream cheese

60 g (¼ cup) mayonnaise

20 g (2 tbsp) ground Parmesan cheese, plus extra for topping

115 g (1 cup) shredded mozzarella

EGG WASH
1 large egg

Splash of water

Sesame seeds, for sprinkling

A few days before baking, feed your starter until bubbly and active. Store at room temperature until ready to use.

MAKE THE DOUGH: Make the recipe for Wreath dough following the method on page 134. During the bulk rise, proceed to the next step.

MAKE THE FILLING: In a large skillet, warm the olive oil over medium-low heat. Sauté the onions until soft and light golden, about 5 to 7 minutes. Add the artichoke hearts and garlic, and cook for 30 seconds. Working in batches, add the spinach and cook slowly to wilt. Season with salt and pepper. Drain away any residual liquid from the spinach and reduce the heat to low. Add the sour cream, cream cheese, and mayonnaise, and stir until creamy. Transfer the filling to a bowl and stir in the Parmesan cheese. Once completely cool, chill the filling until ready to use.

ROLL AND ASSEMBLE: Cut a large sheet of parchment paper and brush lightly with oil. Remove the dough onto the parchment paper. Let rest for 5 to 10 minutes before rolling. With a floured rolling pin, roll the dough into a large rectangle, about 15 × 10 inches (38 × 25 cm), trimming the edges as needed. Spoon the chilled filling down the center, about 4 inches (10 cm) across. You should have a flap of dough on either side. Sprinkle the mozzarella cheese and extra Parmesan on top of the filling.

CUT AND BRAID THE DOUGH: Working with one side at a time, cut 1-inch (2.5-cm) strips down the length of the dough using a lightly oiled pizza wheel or scissors for speedy results. If using a knife, try not to drag the dough as you cut. Repeat, cutting the other side of the dough. Working from the top, overlap the left and right strips to cover the filling. The dough will stretch slightly as you begin the braid. Continue overlapping the dough until you have a full braid. Trim and tuck under the end pieces as needed. Transfer the sheet of parchment paper, with the dough, to a rimmed sheet pan.

Whisk the egg and a splash of water in a small bowl. Brush the dough with the egg wash. Sprinkle generously with sesame seeds, patting them into the dough to coat.

SECOND RISE: Cover the dough and let rest until noticeably puffy, about 1 hour, depending on temperature. Preheat your oven to 425°F (220°C).

BAKE: Bake the dough on the center rack for 30 to 35 minutes, or until rich golden brown. Some of the cheese might bubble and ooze out of the sides while baking, and it will turn crispy all around the edges. Cool for 30 minutes on the sheet pan before cutting into slices. Serve warm or at room temperature with plenty of napkins.

This bread is best enjoyed fresh. Cover with plastic wrap and store at room temperature for up to 1 day.

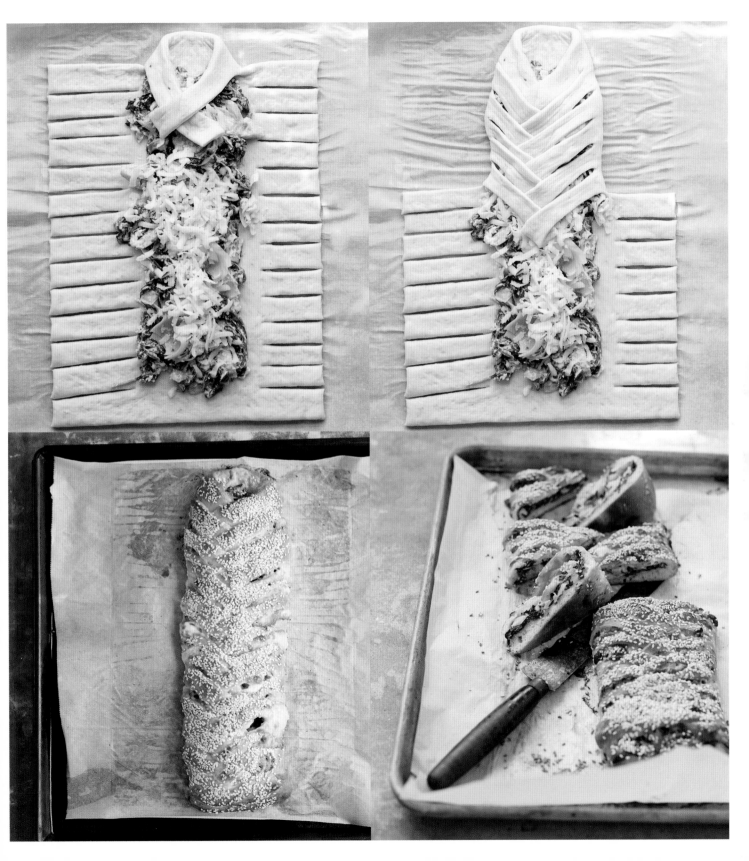

RECIPES *for* LEFTOVER SOURDOUGH STARTER

As part of the feeding process, removing and discarding some of your sourdough starter can oftentimes feel wasteful and counterintuitive. Luckily, there's a practical alternative to dumping it down the drain. Leftover starter can be used in a variety ways beyond making bread, and what's helpful is that you don't have to wait for it to become bubbly and active to use.

The level of sour flavor in these recipes will all depend on the condition of your starter. If it's been sitting in the fridge for 3 weeks, chances are the flavor will be very pungent. My preference is to use recently fed or just-collapsed starter, without too much liquid on the surface. This combination will lend balanced flavor to both sweet and savory recipes. But as always, use your judgment—and your nose.

NOTE: For your reference, the measurements switch to conventional volume for the recipes here and in the next chapter.

CINNAMON SUGAR SOURDOUGH WAFFLES

Makes 4 Waffles

One of the easiest ways to use leftover sourdough starter is to make waffles. Crispy on the outside and light and fluffy in the middle, these cinnamon sugar waffles are incredible. Top with your choice of seasonal fruit, coconut flakes, and a dollop of fresh whipped cream for the ultimate homemade breakfast.

CINNAMON SUGAR
¼ cup (50 g) sugar

1 tsp (3 g) cinnamon

WAFFLES
½ cup (120 g) leftover starter

1 cup (240 ml) milk, whole or 2%

3 tbsp (42 g) unsalted butter, melted, divided

1 large egg

1 cup (120 g) all-purpose flour

1 tbsp (12 g) sugar

2 tsp (10 g) baking powder

½ tsp fine sea salt

Cooking spray, for coating

TOPPINGS
1 cup (165 g) cubed pineapple

Handful of mixed seasonal berries

¼ cup (30 g) coconut flakes

Maple syrup, to serve

Combine the cinnamon and sugar in a shallow bowl.

Preheat your waffle iron according to the manufacturer's instructions. Add the leftover starter, milk, 2 tablespoons (28 g) of melted butter, and egg into a large bowl. Whisk well to combine. Add the flour, sugar, baking powder, and salt and continue to whisk until smooth. If the batter seems too thick, add more milk to thin out the texture. This will all depend on the consistency of your sourdough starter.

Lightly coat the waffle iron with cooking spray. Ladle some of the batter into the waffle iron to fill the pan. Cook for 3 to 5 minutes, or until golden and crisp. Transfer to a cutting board and brush lightly with some of the remaining melted butter. Press the waffle into the cinnamon sugar to coat on both sides. Repeat to cook the rest of the waffles.

To serve, top your waffles with the pineapple, mixed berries, and coconut flakes. Enjoy with sweet maple syrup on the side.

TIP: Once completely cool, these waffles can be frozen for up to 2 months. Cover in plastic wrap and a layer of foil before freezing. Bake frozen at 350°F (180°C) until warmed through.

EASY DIJON-PARSLEY POPOVERS

Makes 6 Large Popovers

Want to know the secret to light and airy popovers? Room temperature batter. I've made plenty of popovers in my day with cold milk, which turned them into custardy muffins, not cloud-like shells. If this happens to you, it's not the end of the world. (My mom happens to like the muffin version.) But to really nail that light, beautiful inside, make sure that the batter feels warm to the touch. These savory popovers are fantastic with soup. You'll need a large popover pan.

1¼ cups (300 ml) milk, whole or 2%

2 tbsp (28 g) unsalted butter, cubed

3 large eggs, at room temperature

½ cup (120 g) leftover starter

1 tbsp (20 g) Dijon mustard

1 tbsp (4 g) finely chopped parsley

¼ tsp garlic powder

½ tsp fine sea salt

Freshly ground black pepper

1 cup (120 g) all-purpose flour

Cooking spray, oil, or melted butter, for coating

Preheat oven to 450°F (230°C). Place a large nonstick popover pan inside to heat up.

In a small saucepan, gently warm the milk and butter over low heat or in the microwave. Allow to cool slightly before adding to the rest of the ingredients.

Meanwhile, crack the eggs into a large bowl. Add the leftover starter, Dijon mustard, parsley, garlic powder, salt, and a few turns of freshly ground black pepper. Whisk well to combine. Gradually pour in the warm milk mixture while continuing to whisk thoroughly. Add the flour and whisk until the batter is thin, frothy, and lump-free.

Remove the hot pan from the oven and lightly coat with cooking spray. Ladle a portion of the batter into the pan, about two-thirds full. It will sizzle. When finished, place the pan on the center rack and reduce the heat to 400°F (200°C). Bake for 40 minutes. The popovers will be beautifully risen and deep golden brown when ready. Serve piping hot. The popovers will begin to deflate as they cool.

SOURDOUGH KEY LIME RICOTTA COOKIES

Makes 3 to 4 Dozen

My best friend makes the best ricotta cookies. We've been eating them since we were kids, sneaking as many as we could from her mom's Christmas cookie tin. I have adapted her original recipe to make them sourdough-friendly, which happens to be the perfect complement to citrusy lime. The texture is delightfully soft, almost cake-like, and sweetened with a quick-and-easy lime glaze. These cookies make great holiday gifts.

COOKIES

8 tbsp (113 g) unsalted butter, softened

1 cup (200 g) sugar

1 large egg

½ cup (120 g) leftover starter

1 cup (125 g) whole milk ricotta

Zest of 1 lime or several key limes

1 tsp (5 ml) pure vanilla extract

3 cups (360 g) all-purpose flour

1 tbsp (15 g) baking powder

½ tsp fine sea salt

LIME GLAZE

¾ cup (90 g) powdered sugar, sifted

Juice of 1 to 2 limes, zest reserved for decoration

Preheat your oven to 350°F (180°C). Line two sheet pans with parchment paper and set aside.

In the bowl of a stand mixer, cream the butter and sugar until light and fluffy, about 3 to 4 minutes. Scrape down the sides of the bowl. Add the egg and mix to combine. With the machine running, add the leftover starter, ricotta, lime zest, and vanilla. Depending on the temperature of your ingredients, the mixture may become lumpy—this is okay.

Meanwhile, whisk the flour, baking powder, and salt together in a large bowl. On low speed, gradually add the dry ingredients and mix until just incorporated. Scrape down the sides of the bowl once more, making sure that there is no flour hiding at the bottom. It will smell wonderful. Cover the bowl in plastic wrap and chill the dough for 30 minutes to 1 hour. Then portion the dough onto your sheet pans using a tablespoon or mini ice cream scoop.

Place both sheet pans into the oven and bake for about 15 to 17 minutes. Rotate the pans and swap racks at the halfway mark for even coloring. When finished, the cookies will be pale yellow with golden bottoms and will feel soft to the touch. Transfer to a wire rack.

For the glaze, sift the powdered sugar into a small bowl. Add the juice of 1 lime and whisk until a smooth glaze forms. If the texture is too thick, add more lime juice as needed until you achieve a pourable consistency.

Once the cookies are completely cool, drizzle some of the glaze over the top. Finish with grated lime zest to decorate.

These cookies will stay fresh for up to 3 to 5 days stored in an airtight container. Alternatively, freeze for up to 2 months by placing unglazed cookies between sheets of parchment paper to prevent sticking.

TIP: Any leftover ricotta can be used to make Sourdough Zeppoles on page 155.

SOURDOUGH ZEPPOLES

Makes About 3 Dozen

Warning: These are highly addictive. Lighter than a donut and similar to a sweet and airy fritter, these sourdough zeppoles will give any carnival food stand a run for their money. The batter includes creamy ricotta and is lightly sweetened with a touch of sugar and vanilla extract. Once fried, they will become perfectly crisp on the outside; you'll have to refrain yourself from gobbling up the whole batch. For best results, make sure that your ingredients are at room temperature before frying.

2 large eggs, at room temperature

1 cup (125 g) whole milk ricotta, at room temperature

½ cup (120 g) leftover starter

½ tsp pure vanilla extract

1 cup (120 g) all-purpose flour

2 tsp (10 g) baking powder

¼ cup (50 g) sugar

Pinch of fine sea salt

6 cups (1.4 L) vegetable oil, for frying

Powdered sugar, to serve

Whisk the eggs, ricotta, leftover starter, and vanilla extract in a large bowl. Add the flour, baking powder, sugar, and salt. Mix with a wooden spoon until just incorporated. The batter will be thick.

Pour the oil into an 8-inch (20-cm) pot. Warm over medium-high heat until it reaches about 360 to 365°F (182 to 185°C). To test whether the oil is hot enough, drop a teaspoon of batter into the pot. If it floats to the top and is surrounded by small bubbles, it's ready. If not, allow the oil to come to temperature and try again.

Using a level tablespoon or mini ice cream scoop, gently lower a few spoonfuls of batter into the hot oil. Fry for about 3 to 4 minutes, turning occasionally, until puffed, deep golden brown, and cooked through in the center. Transfer to a paper towel-lined plate with a large slotted spoon. Adjust the heat if necessary, then finish frying the rest of the batter. *Note:* To prevent the batter from sticking, dip your tablespoon or mini ice cream scoop into the hot oil in between portions.

To serve, dust the zeppoles with powdered sugar while still warm. Enjoy right away.

VARIATIONS: Try swapping the vanilla extract for a drop of Fiori di Sicilia, an aromatic extract with hints of vanilla and citrus. You can easily find this extract in Italian specialty stores and online. You can also roll the dough in cinnamon sugar, in lieu of powdered sugar, while still warm.

PUFFED SOURDOUGH CRACKERS WITH GRUYERE *and* THYME

Makes 3 to 4 Dozen

If you like baking cookies, you should try making homemade crackers. They are essentially the same thing: Roll the dough, cut into shapes, and bake. See? It's more approachable than you'd think. Leftover sourdough starter is perfect for crackers, and these particular beauties puff up and get all crispy when baked. Cold butter and chilled dough are the secret, so make sure that your fridge has a clear shelf on standby. This dough can be made 2 days in advance, wrapped and chilled.

1 cup (120 g) all-purpose flour

½ tsp fine sea salt

¼ tsp garlic powder

¼ cup (60 g) leftover starter

4 tbsp (56 g) unsalted butter, cold, cut into small cubes

8 oz (227 g) Gruyere cheese, grated

2 tbsp (20 g) grated Parmesan cheese

6 sprigs of thyme, leaves picked, plus extra to serve

3 to 4 tbsp (45 to 60 ml) cold water, plus more as needed

Add all of the ingredients to the bowl of a food processor, with 1 tablespoon (15 ml) of water. Pulse until tiny crumbs form. Add more water to bring the dough together, taking care not to overmix. Flatten the dough into a disc, cover with plastic wrap, and chill for at least 30 minutes.

Preheat your oven to 325°F (165°C). Line a sheet pan with parchment paper.

Divide the dough in half. Roll the dough out as thin as possible, about ⅛ inch (3.1 mm). Do this on a sheet of parchment paper to prevent sticking.

Cut the dough into shapes using a 1½-inch (4-cm) mini cookie cutter. Place onto your lined sheet pan, spaced one finger-width apart. Dock the center with a toothpick or the tip of a skinny paintbrush, or leave undocked if you prefer. Chill the dough for 5 to 10 minutes before baking. Meanwhile, gather the scraps, re-roll, and shape again. Repeat with the remaining portion of dough.

Bake the crackers until puffed and light golden brown, about 15 minutes or more, depending on thickness. Cool directly on the sheet pan; they will continue to crisp as they cool. If the crackers are slightly soft in the center, return to a low oven, set to 250°F (130°C), and bake until crisp. Sprinkle with extra thyme leaves to serve.

Once completely cool, store the crackers in an air-tight container for up to 3 days.

BREAK-APART
SESAME SPELT CRACKERS

Serves 4 to 6

In addition to cutout crackers mentioned in the previous recipe, another fun method is to make crackers you can break apart with your hands for a more rustic-style look. This particular dough is exceptionally easy to roll, thanks to the olive oil, and nutty spelt flour and sesame make a wonderful flavor combination. Serve plain as a snack or with your favorite dip. Creamy hummus would be my choice.

1¼ cups (125 g) whole spelt flour

2 tbsp (20 g) sesame seeds

½ tsp fine sea salt

2 tbsp (40 g) honey

¼ cup (60 g) leftover starter

¼ cup (60 ml) olive oil

Add all of the ingredients to a small bowl. Mix with a fork, scraping down the sides of the bowl until the dough comes together. It should feel very soft but not sticky; add more flour as needed. Once combined, wrap and chill the dough overnight, or proceed to the next step.

Preheat your oven to 325°F (165°C).

Divide the dough into 4 equal portions. Cut a large sheet of parchment paper and place onto your work surface. Arrange two pieces of dough on either end of the paper. Working with one piece of dough at a time, roll into a thin rectangle shape, about ¹⁄₁₆ inch (1.6 mm) thick. It doesn't have to look perfect. Roll out the second piece of dough. Use the parchment to transfer the dough to a rimmed sheet pan. *Optional Step:* Using a large knife, gently score the dough into wide strips, to break apart after baking. This is what I've done in the photo. Or simply break into large rustic crackers. Cut a second sheet of parchment and roll out the remaining portions of dough when the first batch goes into the oven.

Bake the crackers for about 15 minutes, depending on thickness. They will darken around the edges and turn light golden brown in the center when ready. They will also feel slightly soft at this point but will crisp as they cool. Once completely cool, break into large pieces.

These crackers keep will keep fresh stored in an air-tight container up to 1 week or more. To freeze, store in between layers of parchment paper for up to 1 month or longer.

TIP: This dough can be made up to two days in advance, and wrapped and chilled until ready to use.

SKILLET GREEK YOGURT FLATBREADS

Makes 8 Flatbreads

Leftover sourdough starter paired with tangy Greek yogurt creates the best homemade flatbreads. They are delightfully soft, and you won't get over how easy they are to make. As the name suggests, flatbreads do not need to rise. But the dough does need to rest for about an hour, so it's easier to roll. These flatbreads freeze beautifully.

Note: The process of making flatbreads is similar to pancakes. Once you see bubbles on the surface, it's time to flip the dough over. To gauge the heat, test a small piece of dough first—that's what I do. Thinly rolled dough will get you soft, bendable flatbreads; thicker rolled dough will create puffy flatbreads.

2½ cups (300 g) all-purpose flour

1 tbsp (12 g) sugar

1 tsp (5 g) fine sea salt

½ tsp baking powder

½ cup (120 g) leftover starter

¼ cup (60 g) Greek yogurt

¼ cup (60 ml) oil

1 to 2 tbsp (15 to 30 ml) warm water

2 tbsp (28 g) unsalted butter, melted

Whisk the flour, sugar, salt, and baking powder together in a large bowl. Add the leftover starter, yogurt, oil, and 1 tablespoon (15 ml) of water. Mix with your hands until a rough dough forms. The dough should feel soft but not sticky. Add more water or flour as needed to get the right texture. Cover with a damp kitchen towel and let rest for 1 hour.

Remove the dough onto a lightly floured work surface. Flatten into a rectangle, and then divide into 8 equal pieces, about 80 grams (2¾ oz) each. Cover with a damp towel.

Working with one piece at a time, roll the dough into a thin circle about 8 inches (20 cm). The exact shape does not need to be perfect—you're looking for something slightly smaller than the width of your skillet. Melt the butter in a small saucepan or in the microwave. Warm a large cast-iron skillet over medium-low heat.

Place the dough into the warm, dry pan and cook for 2 to 3 minutes on one side. When the dough puffs up and has a few bubbles on the surface, brush lightly with some of the melted butter and flip it over. Cook for 1 to 2 minutes on the other side. When finished, brush with more butter and transfer to a cutting board. Wrap in a towel to keep warm. Roll out the next piece of dough and cook the rest of the flatbreads.

These sourdough flatbreads are best enjoyed warm. You can also reheat them in a low oven, about 275°F (140°C), in a foil package. For crispy flatbreads, reheat directly on the center oven rack.

Flatbreads will keep fresh stacked, wrapped, and stored at room temperature for 1 to 2 days. Reheat as indicated above for best texture. To freeze, cover the flatbreads in plastic wrap and foil for up to 3 months.

TIP: After you've made this recipe, try spicing up the dough with different seasonings. Chopped herbs including rosemary and sage are always nice, or try a light dusting of garlic powder and sesame seeds. Sometimes I'll fold in a handful of chopped scallions, which gives the dough a mild onion flavor.

TO ENJOY WITH BREAD

By now, you already know that sourdough needs nothing more than a good bread knife and some peppery olive oil. But to relish every bite, I've compiled several creative and delicious ways for you to enjoy freshly baked or day-old bread. The Fried Artichoke Panzanella (page 168) is a must-make, especially for entertaining. Or, for something sweet, try the Sourdough Brioche con Gelato (page 172), the most decadent ice cream sandwich. Feel free to incorporate sourdough into your own favorite recipes. Bon appétit!

RUM RAISIN BREAD PUDDING

Serves 4 to 6

The best bread pudding you'll ever taste resides in a quaint Italian restaurant on the Upper East Side, called Sfoglia. It's decadent and rich, and it has just a touch of dark rum to deepen the flavor. I tried wrestling the recipe from the chef to no avail, but this version is a close runner-up. I do know that the custard base is cooked briefly to thicken for extra creaminess, a technique that is skipped for most bread puddings. For best results, make sure to use whole milk (not skim, please!) or even a combination of milk and cream. The bottom of the pan is sprinkled with sugar, a trick I learned from Jamie Oliver.

2 cups (480 ml) whole milk

6 large eggs

¼ cup (50 g) sugar, plus extra for sprinkling

Pinch of salt

2 tbsp (28 g) unsalted butter, plus more for coating

2 tbsp (30 ml) dark rum

6 slices day-old Everyday Sourdough (page 26), cubed, about 6 cups (240 g)

Handful of raisins or currants

2 tbsp (30 ml) caramel sauce

Powdered sugar, for sprinkling

For the custard, gently warm the milk in a small saucepan over low heat. Meanwhile, whisk the eggs, sugar, and salt in a medium bowl. Slowly pour the warm milk into the egg mixture, whisking continuously to combine. Then pour the custard back into the pan.

Adjust the heat to medium-low and cook the custard until slightly thick, stirring often to prevent it from scorching on the bottom of the pan, about 10 to 15 minutes. The final texture should be similar to heavy cream, but not thick like pudding. Stir in the butter to melt and add the rum. Strain the custard through a fine-mesh sieve.

Add the bread cubes to a large bowl, along with a handful of raisins. Pour the warm custard over the bread. Toss well to combine. Let the mixture sit for at least 30 minutes to absorb the custard.

Meanwhile, preheat your oven to 350°F (180°C). Generously coat a 9 × 13-inch (23 × 33-cm) pan or oval baking dish with butter. Sprinkle the bottom and sides of the pan with sugar to coat.

Spoon the bread into the baking dish, pouring any leftover custard over the top. The amount of custard left over will depend on how fresh or stale your bread is. Drizzle with the caramel sauce. Bake for about 30 to 35 minutes, or until the bread pudding is set. It should be golden brown, with a soft center. And it will smell divine. Sprinkle with powdered sugar to serve.

WEEKNIGHT TUSCAN RIBOLLITA

Serves 4 to 6

Ribollita is a traditional Italian soup, made with plenty of vegetables and thickened with day-old bread. Although exceptionally flavorful, the soup's texture reminds me of a minestrone bread pudding. Here, I simply serve toasted pumpernickel sourdough on the side, rubbed with a fat clove of garlic for a kick. This soup freezes very well, so make a big batch when you have the time, to defrost any night of the week.

2 tbsp (30 ml) olive oil

1 large onion, diced

1 medium carrot, diced

1 small celery stalk, diced

1 heaped cup (80 g) shredded cabbage

Salt and freshly ground black pepper

1 large clove of garlic, sliced

1 tbsp (16 g) tomato paste

1 to 2 quarts (1 to 2 L) chicken stock, plus more as needed

4 small Yukon Gold or Red Bliss potatoes, diced

1 small bunch of Tuscan kale, shredded

1 cup (250 g) white beans, rinsed and drained

Rustic Pumpernickel (page 88) or a sourdough bread of your choice

1 garlic clove, halved

Extra celery leaves (optional)

Parmesan cheese, to taste

In a large, heavy-bottom pot, warm the olive oil over medium-low heat. Add the onions, carrots, celery, and cabbage, and season with salt and pepper. Sauté until soft, about 5 to 6 minutes. Add the garlic and cook until fragrant.

Add the tomato paste and stir well to dissolve. Pour in 1 quart (1 L) of chicken stock. Bring the soup to a gentle boil, then add the potatoes and kale. Reduce the heat to low and simmer, with the lid tilted, until the vegetables are cooked through, about 30 to 40 minutes. Add more chicken stock as needed or to your liking. Stir in the white beans and warm through.

About 10 minutes before serving, toast or grill the bread, or simply cut into slices. Drizzle with olive oil and rub with a cut clove of garlic while still warm. Season with a touch of salt and pepper. Ladle your soup into bowls and top with extra celery leaves and Parmesan cheese. Serve piping hot with your delicious bread for dunking.

FRIED ARTICHOKE PANZANELLA WITH CRISPY CAPERS *and* MINT

>>>>> *Serves 4* <<<<<

Hand-torn pieces of sourdough, lightly fried in olive oil, are the highlight of this rustic Italian salad. It's also the perfect sponge to soak up all of the zesty flavors, and its crisp texture naturally pairs well with soft, fresh mozzarella cheese. I like to use the Toasted Sunflower sourdough (page 84) for this, but any sourdough will work beautifully. There's something magical about the flavor of sunflower seeds and artichokes together.

¼ cup (60 ml) olive oil, plus more as needed

4 slices Toasted Sunflower (page 88), torn into small pieces, about 4 cups (160 g)

Salt and freshly ground black pepper

2 tbsp (17 g) capers, rinsed and drained

2 cups (250 g) grilled, marinated artichoke hearts, halved

1 cup (120 g) baby mozzarella balls

Handful of fresh mint leaves, cut into ribbons

1 tbsp (8 g) sunflower seeds

In a medium saucepan, heat the olive oil until shimmering hot. Add the bread and lower the heat. Fry the bread, stirring often, until golden brown and crispy, about 10 minutes or more depending on size. Transfer to a paper towel-lined plate. Season lightly with a hint of salt and pepper.

Using the same pan, add the capers and pour in just enough olive oil to cover. Fry the capers, making sure they are completely submerged, until crispy, about 3 to 5 minutes. They will open up like flowers when ready. Transfer to your lined plate. Try one!

Add the artichoke hearts to a large bowl. Gently tear the mozzarella with your hands and add to the artichokes. Toss in the crispy fried bread and mix well to combine. When ready to serve, sprinkle the salad with the mint, sunflower seeds, and crispy capers.

TIP: I use grilled, marinated artichoke hearts, which you can easily find in Italian specialty stores and in the deli section of most grocery stores. But of course, any marinated artichoke hearts will do; choose the best quality that you can find.

OPEN-FACE TOASTED CHEESE *and* TOMATO SANDWICHES

Serves 6

My husband is from South Africa, and one of the first dishes he swooned me with is called "braaibroodjies," which are grilled sandwiches typically enjoyed at "braiis" or BBQs. Imagine thin slices of cheddar with juicy tomato, red onion, and a thin layer of apricot jam, toasted to perfection on an open flame. Staying true to the original but adding a twist, I've made them open-face, cooked under the broiler, topped with fresh basil. Delicious.

6 slices Country Farmhouse White (page 62)

2 to 4 tbsp (40 to 80 g) apricot jam

¼ small red onion, thinly sliced

Small handful of fresh basil, hand torn into small pieces

12 slices white or yellow cheddar

6 slices ripe tomato

Salt and freshly ground pepper

Toast the sliced bread until light golden brown. Arrange on a sheet pan lined with parchment paper.

Spread each slice with a thin layer of apricot jam, a few slices of red onion, basil leaves, and 2 slices of the cheddar cheese. Place a tomato slice on top and season with salt and pepper.

Broil the sandwiches for 2 to 3 minutes or until the cheese is melted and the edges are golden. Sprinkle with a few extra basil leaves to serve.

SOURDOUGH BRIOCHE CON GELATO

In Sicily, you'll find people eating soft brioche buns filled with sweet, creamy gelato right on the beach. I know this because I was one of them! My cousins first introduced me to this grown-up ice cream sandwich, and I've been hooked ever since. To make your own, use the dough recipe for Light and Fluffy Brioche (page 70) and fill with your favorite ice cream or gelato. Don't be shy—it's one of the best things you'll ever try.

1 recipe Light and Fluffy Brioche, shaped into rolls (page 70)

Assorted gelato or ice cream, including chocolate, strawberry, coffee, pistachio, vanilla, and caramel

Sprinkles (optional)

To begin, make the recipe for Light and Fluffy Brioche, but use the variation for rolls (page 70). Once completely cool, slice the rolls in half and fill with 2 scoops or more of your favorite gelato. Coat in sprinkles, if using, and enjoy right away.

FOCACCIA CROUTONS WITH PECORINO *and* DILL

Day-old bread is excellent for croutons. All of those craggy, irregular holes are perfect for soaking up zesty dressings, including the Greek vinaigrette you'll find on page 176. Simply cube up whatever sourdough you have on hand—focaccia is perfect for this—and bake in a moderate oven until golden. I like to sprinkle garlic powder and fresh dill on mine, with a dusting of Pecorino cheese. The flavor is wildly addicting.

5 to 6 cups (200 to 240 g) Basic No-Knead Focaccia (page 92), cubed

2 to 3 tbsp (30 to 45 ml) olive oil

½ tsp garlic powder

2 heaped tbsp (8 g) chopped fresh dill

Pecorino cheese, to taste

Salt and freshly ground black pepper

Preheat your oven to 350°F (180°C)

Arrange the bread cubes on a sheet pan and drizzle with some of the olive oil to coat. Sprinkle with garlic powder, fresh dill, and Pecorino cheese. Season with salt and pepper. Toss gently with your hands, adding more olive oil as needed, until the focaccia is nicely coated.

Bake for 20 to 30 minutes, checking on the croutons at the 15-minute mark. When they are light golden brown and crispy, they're done.

Once completely cool, store in an air-tight container for up to 2 to 3 days.

TIP: Pulse any leftover croutons in a food processor for homemade breadcrumbs. Store at room temperature, or freeze for up to 3 to 6 months.

LIGHT *and* FRESH GREEK SALAD WITH FOCACCIA CROUTONS

Serves 4

If you've made the crispy Focaccia Croutons with Pecorino and Dill on page 175, you've got to try them in this refreshing and healthy salad. It's packed with cool iceberg lettuce, lots of veggies, and feta. The croutons have no problem soaking up the delicious vinaigrette, with punchy flavor packed into every bite.

P.S. I forgot the olives. The plan was to add a good handful of kalamatas, but when I opened the fridge, I only had green olives with pimentos instead. Considering that I was making a salad and not a martini, I forged ahead, sans the salty counterpart. Go ahead and add as many olives to this salad as you'd like.

GREEK VINAIGRETTE

½ cup (120 ml) olive oil

Juice of 1 lemon

1 tbsp (15 ml) red wine vinegar

1 fat garlic clove, smashed

½ tsp dried oregano

2 tbsp (20 g) grated Parmesan cheese

Salt and freshly ground black pepper

SALAD

½ small head of iceberg lettuce, shredded

1 large handful of baby mesclun greens

1 cup (135 g) cherry tomatoes, halved or quartered, depending on size

½ small English cucumber, sliced into rounds

4 small radishes, thinly sliced

½ cup (80 g) chickpeas

½ cup (50 g) kalamata olives (optional)

1 cup (30 g) Focaccia Croutons with Pecorino and Dill (page 175)

¼ cup (50 g) crumbled feta

To make the dressing, add all of the ingredients to an empty jam jar. Season with salt and pepper to taste. Shake well to blend and chill until ready to use. The longer it sits, the more pronounced the garlic flavor will be. You can make this dressing up to 2 days in advance, removing the garlic clove after 1 day.

Add all of the salad ingredients to a large bowl, reserving the crumbled feta. Drizzle with some of the dressing and toss well to combine. The croutons will soak up most of the dressing, so don't be afraid to add more! Right before serving, sprinkle the feta over the top and give it a light toss. Serve at room temperature.

SUMMER TOMATO SALAD

Serves 4

Nothing beats a juicy tomato salad during the height of summer. When combined with good-quality olive oil and fresh herbs, all you need are a few slices of sourdough to mop up all of the delicious flavors. The secret is to let the salad sit for at least 15 minutes or more. The tomatoes will release their juices into the bowl, making the best "sauce" for dunking. My grandpa taught me this trick, and he was famous for his tomato salads. Serve with a few slices of Golden Sesame Semolina (page 87).

P.S. When making this salad, I stumbled across beautiful watermelon radishes at the farmer's market and couldn't resist their vibrant pink and green color. Watermelon radishes are a seasonal treat, so if you are unable to find them, good old red radishes will work, too. It's all about the crunch.

3 to 4 colorful heirloom tomatoes, cut into wedges

Handful of baby heirloom tomatoes, halved

½ celery stick, thinly sliced

1 large watermelon radish or 2 red radishes, thinly sliced

¼ red onion, thinly sliced

2 tbsp (8 g) minced chives

Olive oil, for drizzling

1 tsp (5 ml) red wine vinegar

Salt, to taste

1 tbsp (4 g) celery leaves

½ loaf Golden Sesame Semolina (page 87), cut into slices

Add the tomatoes, celery, radishes, onion, and chives to a large bowl. Drizzle with olive oil to coat, add the vinegar, and season with salt to taste. Toss well to combine. Let the tomato salad sit for at least 15 minutes or more for the flavors to infuse.

When ready to eat, pile your juicy tomato salad into a serving bowl. Sprinkle the celery leaves on top. Arrange the bread slices all around, and serve family-style.

TIP: Use a mandolin to slice the veggies paper-thin. You can also use a vegetable peeler for similar results.

SPICY WHITE BEAN *and* ARUGULA DIP

Serves 4 to 6 as a Light Bite or Appetizer

This creamy white bean dip with baby arugula is the perfect destination for a slice of artisan sourdough. It's not only healthy, but it's incredibly simple to make—just pulse a few times in the blender and you're done. Serve with Overnight Baguette Twists (page 130), which is my recommendation, because the crunchy crust pairs really well with the silky texture of the beans.

1½ cups (375 g) cannellini beans, rinsed and drained

1 small handful of baby arugula

¼ cup (60 ml) olive oil, plus more for drizzling

½ garlic clove, chopped

Pinch of red pepper flakes

Zest of 1 lemon, juice reserved

Salt and freshly ground black pepper

Overnight Baguette Twists (page 130), cut into slices

Add the beans, arugula, olive oil, garlic, red pepper, zest, and juice of half the lemon to a blender. Season generously with salt and pepper. Pulse a few times to combine. The texture should be creamy and rustic. Taste the dip and adjust with more lemon juice or salt and pepper if needed.

Transfer the dip to a small bowl and drizzle with extra olive oil and red pepper flakes. Arrange your sourdough slices on the side, to serve for dipping.

VARIATION: You can also use fresh parsley or cilantro leaves in place of the arugula.

ZESTY GARLIC *and* HERB DIPPING OIL

Serves 2 to 4

There's an Italian restaurant in our neighborhood that serves the most delicious dipping oil with bread upon arrival. I'm always analyzing it to death, dunking and dipping to determine all of the flavors. This version, which includes both fresh and dried herbs, is as close as I'm going to get. The Parmesan at the bottom of the bowl is the best part. And by the way, if you double the recipe, it can be used as a marinade for chicken and shrimp or to drizzle over roasted potatoes.

⅓ cup (80 ml) good-quality olive oil

2 garlic cloves, minced or thinly sliced

Zest of ½ lemon

1 tbsp (4 g) finely chopped parsley

1 tsp (1 g) chopped fresh rosemary

Sprinkle of dried oregano

Sprinkle of red paper flakes

1 heaped tbsp (15 g) ground Parmesan cheese

Salt and freshly ground black pepper

Soft Semolina Breadsticks with Buttery Crumbs (page 126) or Basic No-Knead Focaccia (page 92), for serving

Add all of the ingredients to a small bowl, and mix well to combine. Season generously with salt and pepper. Dunk a piece of bread into the oil to taste, and adjust the seasoning as needed. It should be zesty and flavorful. Serve with breadsticks, focaccia, or your choice of sourdough for dunking.

NOTE: This dipping oil is best prepared right before serving. Garlic oil spoils quickly, so this recipe cannot be made in advance or stored indefinitely.

SMALL-BATCH QUICK JAMS

The benefit of small-batch jams is that you can experiment with a variety of flavors without having to commit to several jars. Plus, this no-fuss approach skips the canning process, allowing you to make artisan-style spreads in 30 minutes or less.

APRICOT *and* VANILLA JAM

Makes about 1 Cup (350 g)

1 lb (450 g) apricots, pitted and chopped

Juice of ½ lemon

1 cup (200 g) sugar

2 vanilla beans or 1 tsp (5 ml) pure vanilla extract

Add the apricots, lemon juice, and sugar to a medium-sized pot. Bring the mixture to a gentle boil, then adjust the heat to low. Meanwhile, halve the vanilla beans lengthwise. Run the tip of a spoon down the length of each half to scrape out the seeds. Add the vanilla, along with the pods, to the pot.

Simmer the apricots, stirring occasionally, until they are soft and broken down, about 20 minutes. As the mixture cooks, skim off any foam that rises to the surface with a small ladle. This will create a clear jam. When your jam is thick and shiny, and coats the back of a spoon without dripping off, it's ready.

For smooth jam, remove from the heat and puree with an immersion blender. For a more rustic texture, mash with a potato masher to your liking. Allow the jam to cool completely, with the vanilla pods tucked in to infuse. Portion into jars and keep refrigerated for up to 2 weeks. Serve with your favorite sourdough bread.

CHERRY BALSAMIC JAM

Makes about 1 Cup (350 g)

1 lb (450 g) frozen pitted cherries

1 cup (200 g) sugar

Juice of ½ lemon

1 to 2 tsp (5 to 10 ml) balsamic vinegar

Tip the whole cherries into a medium-sized pot. Add the sugar, lemon juice, and 1 teaspoon (5 ml) of vinegar and give it a good stir. Cook over medium-low heat, until the sugar is dissolved and the cherries start to soften, about 10 minutes. Increase the heat and bring the cherries to a gently simmer. Continue to cook, stirring occasionally, for about 20 minutes. Skim off any foam that rises to the surface.

Remove the pot from the heat, and puree with an immersion blender until smooth. Return to the stove and simmer until the mixture thickens slightly, about 5 minutes. Once completely cool, taste the jam and add the remaining 1 teaspoon (5 ml) of vinegar, if you prefer. Ladle into a small jar or container. Refrigerate for up to 2 weeks. Serve with your favorite sourdough bread.

TECHNIQUES

This section is your go-to resource for shaping and scoring sourdough. Each technique is accompanied by step-by-step photos to help you visually understand the process. After all, a picture is worth a thousand words. . . .

HOW TO SHAPE ROUND LOAVES

Remove the dough from the bowl onto a floured surface.

Starting at the top, fold the dough over and press it down gently toward the center.

Give the dough a slight turn, and fold over the next section.

Repeat until you have come full circle.

(continued)

HOW TO SHAPE ROUND LOAVES (CONT.)

Flip the dough over and let rest for 5 to 10 minutes.

With floured hands, cup the dough and tuck the sides underneath.

Pull the dough toward you in a circular motion to tighten the shape.

Place the dough into a lined bowl or proofing basket, seam side up.

HOW TO SHAPE OVAL LOAVES

Remove the dough from the bowl onto a floured surface.

Starting on the left (or right) side, stretch the dough and fold it over toward the center.

Repeat on the other side.

Stretch and fold the dough from the bottom.

(continued)

Repeat on the top.

Flip the dough over and let rest for 5 to 10 minutes.

With floured hands, pull the dough toward you to tighten its shape.

Place the dough into your proofing basket, seam side up.

HOW TO SHAPE SANDWICH LOAVES

On a lightly floured surface, gently flatten the dough to release any large air bubbles.

Roll the dough into a log, tucking the ends underneath.

Let rest for 5 to 10 minutes and then tighten the dough's shape.

Place the dough into a loaf pan, seam side down.

HOW TO SHAPE ROLLS

Divide the dough into equal portions.

Gather the ends and pinch to seal.

Flip the dough over, cup it with your palm, and roll it into a ball until it begins to tighten.

Place the dough on a sheet pan.

HOW TO STRETCH AND FOLD THE DOUGH

With lightly wet hands, grab a portion of the dough and stretch it upward.

Fold the dough over toward the center of the bowl.

Give the bowl a one-quarter turn and repeat.

Continue until you have come full circle to complete 1 set, or 4 folds.

SCORING PATTERNS

Scoring sourdough is an art that takes practice but is also a lot of fun to do. For best results, use the tip of small, sharp knife or a razor blade for more intricate patterns. And as previously mentioned, you can always practice on a ball of playdough before trying your hand on the real thing.

Straight line: Make one 6- to 7- inch (15-to 18-cm) cut down the length of the dough, about ¼ inch (6.3 mm) deep.

Half-moon: Make one curved, off-center cut, using minimal pressure at the top and base but becoming deeper toward the center, about ¼ inch (6.3 mm).

Starburst: Create a half-moon shape, then score 4 shallow, diagonal cuts on the opposite side of the curved cut.

Leaf shapes: Make a straight line down the length of the dough, and then score 2 rows of V-shaped cuts about 1 inch (2.5 cm) long on either side.

Bird wings: Make 2 to 3 vertical rows of V-shaped cuts, about 1½ to 2 inches (3 to 5 cm) long.

Cross cut: Make four shallow 4-inch (10-cm) long cuts at 3, 6, 9, and 12 o'clock.

SOURCE LIST

LE CREUSET

Quality enameled cast-iron cookware and Dutch ovens

www.lecreuset.com

KING ARTHUR FLOUR

America's oldest flour company, providing top-quality baking products, including unbleached flour, whole-grain flours, a wide range of specialty flours, Harvest Grains Blend, Artisan Bread Topping, extracts, and bread storage bags

www.kingarthur.com

BOB'S RED MILL

Trusted supplier of high-quality flours, 10-grain hot cereal mix, and seeds

www.bobsredmill.com

AMAZON

A wide range of enamel roasting pans for baking, proofing baskets, cotton kitchen towels, digital scales, bench scrapers, scoring tools, La Baleine fine sea salt, and digital and oven thermometers

www.amazon.com

COSTCO

Bulk dried fruit, a wide variety of nuts, and enough parchment paper to last you a lifetime

www.costco.com

ACKNOWLEDGMENTS

THANK YOU TO:

My favorite, lovable boys, Dillon, Jake, and Johan, for your undeniable support and patience, and for being there for me without question. We did it! I couldn't be more grateful. Aren't you guys going to miss the kitchen all covered in flour and dough?

Mom and Dad, the best parents in the world, for helping me in more ways than you can ever imagine. Mom, I can't believe you bake sourdough now. Dad, thank you for wrangling the boys and supplying endless amounts of coffee.

My giant, bread-loving family, who are always ready and willing to sample a slice. Gotta love that honest critique. Eric, thank you for my brand-new oven and stove! (Now what about the rest of my kitchen?)

The entire team at Page Street Publishing, for giving me the opportunity to share my story. This was an incredible project from start to finish, and I am forever thankful.

Sarah Monroe, my editor extraordinaire, for baking along and keeping me sane. A million hugs to you, because "thank you" doesn't even cut it.

Jade Gedeon, your illustrations are exceptional and brought my vision to life. If only my stick figures could look as good as your work!

My fantastic recipe testers, Lia Teixeira, Margie Evans, and Martine Resta, for taking the time out of their busy lives to help out.

My readers near and far. You are a beautiful, passionate group of people who continue to inspire me every day.

Ross Charap, for always taking the time to talk to me and offer sound advice. Connie would be proud.

And finally, Celia Callow and Priscilla. Without you girls, this book would not exist.

ABOUT THE AUTHOR

EMILIE RAFFA is a graduate of the International Culinary Center and author of *The Clever Cookbook.* Her work has been featured online and in several print publications, including *O, the Oprah Magazine; Redbook;* and *Clean Eating.* Her popular blog, The Clever Carrot, offers humor and clever tips for a healthy and balanced lifestyle. Emilie lives on Long Island with her husband and two boys. This is her second book.

INDEX